USELESS
BEAUTY

USELESS
BEAUTY

Ecclesiastes through the Lens
of Contemporary Film

ROBERT K. JOHNSTON

Baker Academic
Grand Rapids, Michigan

© 2004 by Robert K. Johnston

Published by Baker Academic
a division of Baker Publishing Group
P.O. Box 6287, Grand Rapids, MI 49516-6287
www.bakeracademic.com

Second printing, August 2005

Printed in the United States of America

Library of Congress Cataloging-in-Publication Data
Johnston, Robert K., 1945–
    Useless beauty : Ecclesiastes through the lens of contemporary film / Robert K. Johnston.
        p.   cm.
    Includes bibliographical references and index.
    ISBN 0-8010-2785-3 (pbk.)
    1. Bible. O.T. Ecclesiastes—Criticism, interpretation, etc. 2. Motion pictures—Religious aspects—Christianity. I. Title.
    BS1475.52.J64 2004
    223′.806—dc22   2004007267

In memory of
David Alan Hubbard
and
Roland E. Murphy,
mentors and friends who deepened my love for
the Book of Ecclesiastes

CONTENTS

ILLUSTRATIONS

PREFACE

The very commonness of everyday things harbors the eternal marvel
and silent mystery of God.

> Karl Rahner, *Karl Rahner in Dialogue:
> Conversations and Interviews, 1965–1982*

The Septuagint translation of the Book of Exodus speaks of
those who "saw the voice" of the Lord.* What a provocative
image! Here in a nutshell is the intention of this book—to help
readers "see" the voice of the Lord. The hard, paradoxical reality of
life as described in the pages of Ecclesiastes is portrayed visually in
movies such as *American Beauty* and *Monster's Ball*. These films, by
providing a parallel picture to what is described in Ecclesiastes, bring
to life an enigmatic portion of Scripture for both Christians and
Jews. In this book, we will be taking Ecclesiastes to the movies.

To change the metaphor, the "useless beauty" portrayed in a select
group of movies that came out recently will be our eyeglasses and
hearing aids in this book. Their stories can enable us to comprehend
what Ecclesiastes describes as joyful life in our vain (useless, short,

---

*This was the Greek translation of the Old Testament used in Jesus' day. The text
is Exodus 20:18 ("witnessed the thunder and lightning" [NRSV]). A related text is
Moses' sermon in Deuteronomy 4:12, which is based on the Exodus passage. It also
refers to "seeing . . . a voice."

11

absurd) existence. In turn, the Book of Ecclesiastes can help us to see more clearly what these filmmakers are presenting. This book is therefore an attempt at two-way dialogue. Two edgy sources of wisdom—contemporary movies and Ecclesiastes—one ancient and one postmodern, will be put into conversation to explore what if any meaning can be found within life's contradictions.

Life is too often unfair. We cannot know what the future holds. Death is the one unifier. And yet life also offers itself as a fragile gift from the Creator. It begs to be enjoyed for what it is. How can these opposite realities be understood? Both cinema and Old Testament wisdom texts provide us with "answers."

Such a dialogue is questioned by many. Some think the Bible is irrelevant or heavy-handed with respect to film. Others think film is superfluous or even dangerous to faith. This book, however, invites a conversation. Although two-way dialogue is the goal, the conversation will typically move from film to Scripture and only then the reverse. One's theological understanding is of ultimate importance, to be sure. But for the sake of both the integrity of a film's portrayal of reality and the strengthening of one's own faith, theological judgment will follow our "seeing" of the films.

Useless Beauty invites a relatively new form of critical dialogue—a fairly recent hermeneutic vis-à-vis the Bible. It proposes to move from movie to sacred text and only then to reverse the interpretative flow and invite a two-way conversation. The dialogue with culture can and should be a robust one for a person of faith. This is the experience of growing numbers of spiritually sensitive filmgoers. The multiplex is informing the church and the synagogue as well as the reverse. But seldom does theologically informed film criticism allow for such an inductive conversation.[1] Instead, theological criticism more commonly bases its judgments on "truth" already understood.[2] This book should be viewed as one effort to redress this situation.[3]

This study is written as an exercise in attentiveness, in observing more carefully biblical text, contemporary film, and life itself. Some in the Christian community will no doubt question the appropriateness of giving one's attention to some of the movies chosen. Should anyone, they will ask, choose to view the explicit violence and sexuality depicted in *Monster's Ball*? But life's messiness knows no borders and cries out for meaning. It will not be ignored. More-over, Scripture itself is realistic in its depiction of the underbelly of life. (Think of David and Bathsheba; or the rape of Dinah, Jacob's daughter, and the slaughter that ensued.) The Bible refuses to white-wash life. Attention to life's struggles as depicted on screen and in biblical text can help us attend to life's paradoxical reality—its joys that are found within its pain.

It will, of course, be helpful for readers of this book to view ahead of time the movies discussed. In this way, nuances in the movies will not be missed, and surprises will not be spoiled. It will also prove helpful for readers to read the short text of Ecclesiastes. Otherwise, the inclusion of texts within a discussion of a movie might seem more like the practice of proof texting used in a bad sermon than occasions for dialogue and personal reflection.

Having said this, I tried to write the book so that someone can follow the argument even if he or she has not seen a particular movie or read the biblical text. The book can, in this way, function as an invitation to visit the local Blockbuster and/or read this short Old Testament wisdom book for further reflection. Themes of life and death, choice and chance, loneliness and connection, God's absence and presence fill the pages of *Useless Beauty*, just as they permeate our present cultural landscape. Ours is a time when we feel threatened by chaos and contradictions. Yet it is also a time of fragile joy and hope. *Useless Beauty* provides one exploration of this paradoxical spirit of our age. As such it serves as an introduction for those who desire further reflection on either biblical or film texts.

This volume divides roughly into two sections. The discussion opens by putting the conversation into a wider cultural framework and by providing an overview of the Book of Ecclesiastes. This is followed by a chapter that describes the cultural context of the 1950s and 1960s, when existential thought held sway. The goal is to see how both Ecclesiastes and the contemporary films of Akira Kurosawa and Woody Allen were interpreted in its light.

These initial, more deductive chapters are then followed by six inductive studies of contemporary filmmakers, together with one or more of their most significant movies. *American Beauty, Magnolia, Run Lola Run, Monster's Ball, Signs, Election,* and *About Schmidt* are considered in depth, while other movies by the same creators are at times briefly discussed to illumine central themes. These observations are in turn put into conversation with texts from Ecclesiastes to bring to light the "saddest happy endings" of these bittersweet films. How are we to understand the relationship between chance and choice, death and life, work and significance, evil and God? How might Ecclesiastes assist viewers in this process?

The book concludes with a reflection on similar themes taken from the Book of Ecclesiastes itself. The final chapter's intent is to show how this most "dangerous" book, as one medieval commentator called Ecclesiastes, might add insight and depth to the wisdom that contemporary filmmakers are providing.

Useless Beauty seeks to help readers better understand the relevance of film as a tool for theological thought and reflection in the twenty-first century by helping them "see" the voice of the Lord in one of the Old Testament's most enigmatic of books, Ecclesiastes. By putting movies, biblical text, and contemporary context into a dialogue, this book seeks to elicit the continuing power of the biblical text for faith and life today.

ACKNOWLEDGMENTS

The initial ideas for this book were first developed at a conference held at the University of Cambridge, Cambridge, England, in September 2000. It was presented by Fuller Seminary's Reel Spirituality Institute as part of a larger international festival of the arts. I wish to thank Jeremy Begbie, the organizer of the festival, and Craig Detweiler, then codirector with me of Reel Spirituality, for their help with this project. The theme for the event was "Cinematic Wisdom and the Book of Ecclesiastes." One hundred and fifty people crammed into historic Peterhouse Theatre to watch movies, listen to the text of Ecclesiastes being read, and engage in strenuous and productive dialogue. As participants laughed and cried together, this experimental colloquy convinced me that the wisdom embedded in some contemporary film and that found in the Old Testament text of Ecclesiastes had real affinities. I was particularly thankful for the comments of Mary Whybray, the wife of the late Old Testament scholar R. Norman Whybray, who spoke with passion about the rightness of the project and her sadness that her husband could not be present to participate in what he would have enjoyed so much. It was also at that conference that my friend and current codirector of the Reel Spirituality Institute, Barry Taylor, made the suggestion that the dialogue reminded him of Elvis Costello's song "All This Useless Beauty." Here was the genesis of this book's title.

15

Subsequently, I have refined material used in this book through lectures at Oberlin and Westmont colleges; in a plenary address for the Conference on Christianity and Literature, Western section; and in my presidential address to the American Theological Society in April 2004. I have also taught the material in this book to several hundred students at Fuller Seminary, where interest in theology and film has exploded over the last half dozen years. Much of what follows is the direct result of my dialogue with these students. I wish in particular to thank my class in the fall of 2003. They were given an early draft of most of the chapters. Their criticism and suggestions improved the book immensely.

Thanks, as well, to my editor and friend, Robert N. Hosack. This is the third book on which I have worked with him in the area of theology and film. Though the topic is now of great interest to many (one needs only to say *The Passion*), Bob was willing to encourage this dialogue even when many thought it would create limited if any interest.

Finally, I wish to thank my wife, Catherine Barsotti, who has been an active collaborator in most of my theology and film projects and who regularly writes and co-teaches in this area with me. Her encouragement, critique, and love mean everything to me.

A BATTERED OPTIMISM

Ecclesiastes and Our Contemporary Context

I tell New Yorkers they have to learn how to mourn and cry, even while
at the same time celebrating Christmas with more enthusiasm.

Rudolph Giuliani, during the Christmas season following 9/11

In his 1996 song, "All This Useless Beauty," Elvis Costello critiques
the repeated attempts to turn life into a "sweetheart, plaything,
or pet." After all, "Nonsense prevails, modesty fails / Grace and
virtue turn into stupidity." And yet Costello plaintively asks, "What
shall we do, what shall we do with all this useless beauty?"[1] Costello
is not alone in voicing such negations and affirmation. In fact, these
juxtaposed reflections on life are becoming a hallmark of postmodern
Western society.

Many of the young see the modern era as over, even as their
middle-aged parents plunge ahead in a futile attempt to make things
perfect. Those under thirty often see their parents' attempts at creating the ideal life as little more than the construction of personal

towers of Babel, monuments to hubris that should be judged as such. Those who grew up in the period of peace following World War II have too often believed that they have the answers or can find them (JFK taught them to believe they could achieve anything, even jump over the moon, as their nursery rhymes had fantasized). As "modern" Americans, our wisdom seems almost beyond question. We can know the truth, and the truth will set us free. Yet our obsession with achievement, wisdom, wealth, and status, with bigger houses and the better life, with more gadgets and playthings, betrays our rhetoric. It has left us shriveled and panting, our marriages in shambles, our schedules and commute times unacceptable. Kids know this even if we sometimes don't. They reject much of what we stand for, much like the wider world judges America as the obnoxious rich kid on the block.

And yet as the millennium has turned, some young people have discovered that however messy and problematic life is (or perhaps because it is messy and problematic), it also remains precious. Life is something to be nurtured in its beauty and fragility. Modernity's rationality is being called into question by the next generation, and a new wisdom is emerging—from the midst of life itself. Rather than bemoan or fight life's paradox, a growing number of the younger generation are choosing to celebrate the good they find, even if it is always interwoven with evil. There is a developing recognition of a basic contradiction in life but one that nevertheless includes meaning and hope. Calvin Klein, the always savvy marketer, was one of the first to recognize this trend as he updated the names of his latest perfumes to express the evolving mood of his customers. When the boomers were young, he sold them Obsession. As they aged, he sold them Eternity and more recently Escape. Now their children are buying Contradiction.[2]

Ecclesiastes: A "Dangerous" Book

Given the futility of our struggle to turn life into our "plaything," what should we say about the useless beauty that life nevertheless provides? Is it grounds for celebration and enjoyment, even during our brief and futile lives? Elvis Costello's question about life—how to respond to its concurrent vanity and beauty—is, of course, a perennial question. It has been asked again and again. The ancient Babylonian *Epic of Gilgamesh* reflected on life's paradoxes as did the Egyptian *Dispute over Suicide*. But nowhere has it been presented with the depth and poignancy of the Old Testament Book of Ecclesiastes. As its writer, Qoheleth (this Hebrew word is the author's self-designation, meaning "one who assembles"), recognized, though fanatics may try to discern a world order, whether moral or religious, it will always elude their grasp.[3] Death is the great leveler. Life is too often unfair. We cannot know what the future holds. And yet life offers itself as a gift from the Creator. Life begs to be enjoyed for what it is, even given its contradictions.

But just as older Americans struggle to make sense of the paradoxical thoughts of today's emerging postmodern generation, so traditional interpreters of Ecclesiastes have struggled to understand the contradictory thoughts of this enigmatic book. How can the writer say, on the one hand, that "those who have never been born" are "better off," for they "have never seen the injustice that goes on in the world," and yet reflect a few pages later, "But anyone who is alive in the world of the living has some hope; a live dog is better off than a dead lion" (Eccles. 4:3; 9:4)? Such concurrent reflections of both despair and hope make no sense, and yet we realize from our own experience that they make all the sense in the world.

Medieval Old Testament scholars called Ecclesiastes one of the Bible's "two dangerous books." (The other was the Song of Songs with its overt sensuality.) Though its trenchant observations on life reveal a fragile joy—a useless beauty—its paragraphs also brim over with a cynicism and even a despair that seem out of place in the Bible's grand narrative.[4] "Nonsense prevails, modesty fails. / Grace and virtue turn into stupidity." And yet what of life's useless beauty? Is such a conclusion simply fatalistic hedonism, a Hebrew contextualization of "eat, drink, and be merry, for tomorrow we die"? Or might we combine these contradictory trajectories of pessimism and wonder in other ways?

Fascination with this short book in the Hebrew and Christian Scriptures has continued throughout the centuries, for the questions it poses have an enduring appeal. Artists in particular have found Qoheleth's reflections captivating. Herman Melville, in *Moby Dick,* described Ecclesiastes as "the truest of all" books, this "fine-hammered steel of woe."[5] The novelist Thomas Wolfe described Ecclesiastes as "the greatest single piece of writing I have ever known." George Bernard Shaw compared it to Shakespeare. Ernest Hemingway was fascinated by the book. His novel *The Sun Also Rises* uses as an epigraph the book's opening poem. A character in John Updike's Rabbit trilogy describes Ecclesiastes as "the Lord's last word." And U2 used this short book as inspiration for its song "The Wanderer."[6]

The Virginia Museum of Fine Arts displayed an exhibit of contemporary sculpture and installation art in the spring of 2000 titled *Vanitas: Meditations on Life and Death in Contemporary Art.* Using Ecclesiastes 1:2–4 as the epigraph for his exhibition catalogue (printing the text in white against a black background), the curator, John Ravenal, began his remarks, saying, "The theme of *Vanitas* concerns one of life's fundamental tensions, between the enjoyment of earthly pleasures and accomplishments and the awareness of their inevitable loss." After referencing seventeenth-century Dutch still-life painting, which often contained sustained visual expression of this theme, he commented:

> It is only natural that this venerable subject, which for so long has epitomized human self-reflection, should resurface now. The historic milestone of a changing millennium encourages both backward and forward glances as we take stock of the human condition, assessing distance traveled and progress yet to be made. A host of pressing global issues—including frequent outbreaks of civil and international warfare, widening polarization between rich and poor, and pervasive environmental destruction—make it impossible to avoid the perception that conflict and crisis are hallmarks of contemporary life.[7]

In ways that echo the Book of Ecclesiastes, the exhibit by fourteen contemporary international artists juxtaposed beauty and death (darkness, loss, and decay). The artists recognized that these are not only perennial opposites but also facets of the same experience.

Rather than stifle creativity, this bittersweet awareness had spurred these artists.

It is not just the music of Elvis Costello and U2, the fiction of John Updike, and the art of selected contemporary sculptors that have turned recently to the theme of Ecclesiastes, however. Contemporary filmmakers have found its concerns to be central to their understanding of life as well. Some "prophets" of the modern period—Akira Kurosawa *(Ikiru)* and Woody Allen *(Crimes and Misdemeanors)*—dealt with the theme of life's vanity and yet the need for joy. But as the new millennium has dawned, films such as *Magnolia, Run Lola Run, Life as a House, Moulin Rouge, My Name Is Joe, Monster's Ball, Signs, George Washington,* and *About Schmidt* have taken up this contradiction with renewed vigor, using as a central theme life's faint joy amid and within what is bleak and unpromising.

There is perhaps no better example than the 1999 Academy Award–winning movie *American Beauty,* which calls into question our contemporary obsession with producing "beauty" while simultaneously suggesting that there is another more fragile beauty that is present for those who have eyes to see it. Lester's voice-over at the movie's beginning and end serves in a similar way to the opening and closing poems of Ecclesiastes, bookending what happens in between: "It's hard to stay mad when there's so much beauty in the world. . . . I can't feel anything but gratitude for every single moment of my stupid little life."

Ecclesiastes and Contemporary Movies

Contemporary film, rather than being a deterrent to faith, can provide the spectacles, the eyeglasses, to clarify our vision as we look at Ecclesiastes' enigmatic text. In saying this, I am making three simultaneous claims. First, the sages, the wise men and women of our age, are often filmmakers. They are the ones who are creating the root metaphors by which we seek to live. They are the ones who are providing our read on reality, our informing visions, our stories and myths. "Seen any good movies lately?" is a common question for most of us.

Second, interpreters always read texts (view films) in light of their own understanding.[8] The era of seeing total "objectivity" as a value when reading a text is over. A text is "objective" in the sense that it has been created by someone and given to us, not created by us. But this text must also be interpreted by readers who bring their visions and perspectives to bear on the material. Such a focus on the reader/viewer need not cancel out one's concern for the text as text. Rather, it puts the text into a helpful conversation with the reader of it.

Finally, we are at a propitious moment for understanding Ecclesiastes afresh, for the paradoxes and contradictions recognized as central by postmodernity are central as well to this Old Testament book. Qoheleth's cultural read has come full circle. He too lived in a time of outward affluence and saw both an exaggeration of the inequalities between rich and poor and a growing instability for the privileged. As Qoheleth recognizes, "What has happened before will happen again. . . . There is nothing new in the whole world" (1:9). Though we read Ecclesiastes through our contemporary eyeglasses, could it be that these glasses are helping us to see something of the original paradox that Qoheleth observed so well? Such is the contention of the present book.

Religion and film criticism from a Christian perspective has often judged films according to a standard of truth already and independently understood. The exercise of theology and film criticism has been viewed as largely a second order analytical reflection about themes independently understood based on the Christian tradition. The conversation has thus tended to be unidirectional, flowing from faith to film, church to Hollywood, theology to the movies. What has been judged more fundamental, theology, has been given epistemological priority. But there is another possibility: We might profitably reverse the "hermeneutical flow." This phrase belongs to Larry Kreitzer, an Oxford University professor who has argued in a series of four books on literature, film, and theology that theological interpretation can helpfully move from film and novel to the Bible, not just from the Bible to film.[9]

Philip Yancey, in his best-selling book from the 1990s, *The Jesus I Never Knew*, does just that, discovering in a dozen Jesus movies a recognition of Jesus' real humanity that had escaped him as he grew up reading the Bible in a conservative Christian context.[10] Similarly, Robert Jewett, a leading New Testament professor, in his book *St. Paul Returns to the Movies*, entertains the notion that "certain movies afford deeper access to the hidden heart of Paul's theology than mainstream theologians like myself have been able to penetrate."[11] Jewett's beef is with Pauline scholars in the West who have misunderstood, he believes, the discussion of grace in the Book of Romans. Interpreters of that book have understood grace in terms of a "guilt" needing individual forgiveness rather than a corporate "shame" needing to be overcome. Jewett believes that our cultural blinders have kept us from interpreting the text as originally intended by Paul. To move beyond our impasse, we need a new set of stories with a different informing vision. He believes that Hollywood movies provide that alternative perspective, giving us new spectacles to help us see beyond the fixations of our Western, individualistic mind-set.

The parallel proposition of the present book is that contemporary movies afford interpreters a deeper access to Ecclesiastes' center of power and meaning than does much of mainstream Old Testament scholarship. A few scholars have revealed a willingness to accept paradox and contradiction as the heart of Ecclesiastes. But nonlinear thinking is a recent development, and it has been hard to grasp by most of those schooled in the twentieth-century Western world.

Movies function as modern-day parables, giving us fresh eyes to see and ears to hear. Conversely, the paradoxes and tensions found in Ecclesiastes can provide interpretive lenses for the viewing of movies. The conversation is most productive and vibrant if it is two-way. Movies and biblical text can provide mutually penetrating perspectives on how viewers/readers hold on to themes of despair and joy concurrently. This mutual conversation holds the promise of helping us to celebrate "all this useless beauty."

As the millennium dawned, several of us who teach or study at Fuller Theological Seminary organized a conference in Cambridge, England, to explore just such a hypothesis. The conference was held in September 2000 as part of a larger festival exploring "Theology through the Arts" (the name of the event). One hundred and fifty people crammed into the historic Peterhouse Theatre to watch *Liar, Liar; Pleasantville; My Name Is Joe;* and *American Beauty* and then to put these disparate movies into conversation with Ecclesiastes. A special edition of that biblical text had been prepared by the British and Foreign Bible Society, making use of the Good News Bible translation.* We read portions of the text prior to viewing a particular movie and then again after viewing it, before we began our discussion. The dialogue flowed insightfully between film and Bible.

One particularly memorable moment took place after the viewing of *Pleasantville* when Old Testament wisdom scholar Jo Bailey Wells, then chaplain of Claire College, read the Good News translation of the ninth chapter of Ecclesiastes: "Go ahead—eat your food and be happy; drink your wine and be cheerful. It's all right with God. Always look happy and cheerful. Enjoy life with the one you love, as long as you live the *useless* life that God has given you in this world. Enjoy every *useless* day of it" (9:7–9, emphasis added). Jo could hardly be heard over the laughter that spontaneously erupted after both mentions of life's uselessness. Yes, we are to enjoy life—in all its living Technicolor. But it is also true that there is no larger meaning we can assign to our effort. Life is "useless," "vain" (the Hebrew word is *hebel*). Life is "not supposed to be like anything," as Bud told his mom (and us, the viewers) at the end of the movie *Pleasantville.* Life simply cannot be manipulated to produce an antiseptic, *Leave It to Beaver,* sitcom existence. Nor is that something worth striving for. Life is random, and yet life is precious and wonderful too. It is both at the same time, and we as conferees were shocked into an awareness of this contradiction in all its starkness. Given the paradox, there was little left to do but laugh . . . or cry (something we also did after seeing *My Name Is Joe*).

To hold together joy and sorrow, meaninglessness and meaningfulness is a vexing problem in any age. But it was particularly difficult during most of the twentieth century, given our philosophi-

---

*This book will make use of this same Good News Bible translation in order that Qoheleth's ancient text may be heard with power and freshness.

cal commitment to a linear epistemology. We came to bel
when understood clearly, everything would or could fol
cally and orderly without friction or intrusion. But as modernity's
epistemological bankruptcy became more and more evident, our
culture turned elsewhere for models by which to understand existence, including the arts.

Jeremy Begbie, who organized the "Theology through the Arts"
festival, is a professionally trained musician who teaches theology at
both Cambridge University and the University of St. Andrews. In a
book he edited, *Beholding the Glory,* which was prepared specifically
for the conference, Begbie offered an example of how music can
provide new interpretive perspectives.[12] First, visualize the colors
red and yellow. If they are painted on top of each other, either the
two colors will merge into orange, or if the paint of one is already
dry, the second color will simply blot out the other. Applied to
a reading of Ecclesiastes, "meaninglessness" will simply blot out
"meaningfulness," or it will compromise any vibrancy and wonder
meaningfulness might possess.[13]

But, says Begbie, if we turn to music rather than to art, we note
an alternate interpretive reality. When two notes are played together,
they do not merge into something else, nor does one obliterate
the other. Rather, the two notes fill up the entire aural space while
remaining distinct. They "interpenetrate" each other, sounding
"through one another" in such a way that a third thing emerges, a
chord. This chord contains both differentiation and union. Here is
an alternate conceptual tool, a new model or hermeneutical strategy
for dealing with what has otherwise proven intractable. Begbie suggests that music can provide if not "eyeglasses" then a "hearing aid"
to help us better understand biblical theology. In the same way, the
present book centers on the content, or themes, of recent movies as
a theological resource.

A Brief Biblical-Theological Rationale

Common grace—the work of the Holy Spirit throughout and
within all creatures and creation—is the theological basis for this

book's reflection. Unfortunately, it has too often been a neglected topic among Christians. (A recent survey of evangelical seminary students and professors, for example, ranked it as receiving significantly less attention in their seminary's curriculum than matters of Scripture or the mission of the church.)[14] When mentioned, common grace has typically been restricted to clarifying our common sinfulness and/or protecting humankind from itself. That is, God's grace, when experienced outside the church and without direct reference to Jesus Christ, has largely been understood defensively and instrumentally. Little has been said with regard to the Spirit's positive role in culture's outworking, except to assert that, of course, the Spirit is present wherever truth, beauty, or goodness reside. What Jürgen Moltmann has labeled "the divine energy of life," which is experienced throughout creation, has been neglected in most Christian theology in favor of a focus solely on the redemptive Spirit of Christ.[15] What is, in fact, meant to be united within one Spirit—the Spirit's work in creation and in redemption—has been bifurcated, and then one foci has been largely dismissed.

Yet the Spirit's common grace continues to assert itself in both creation and creature. The Spirit not only convicts but also convinces, not only preserves but also provides.[16] As the spiritual proclaims, "He's got the whole world in his hands." My favorite poem is Elizabeth Barrett Browning's "Aurora Leigh":

> Earth's crammed with heaven,
> And every common bush afire with God;
> But only he who sees, takes off his shoes—
> The rest sit round it and pluck blackberries.[17]

One might imagine that God's creative, life-giving presence would have been developed by Christians into a vital, life-affirming theology of common grace. But such has not been the case, despite both our continuing experience of the Spirit's presence in our lives and the consistent witness of Scripture to that reality. Common grace needs to find its proper place once again within the canons of Christian theology. It is not the whole story, yet neither should it be disparaged.

Consider the psalmist's words in Psalm 147:18: "He gives a command, and the ice melts; he sends the wind [or "spirit"—the Hebrew word *ruach* can mean both], and the waters flow." Or recall Paul's words to the people of Lystra: "You should turn . . . to the living God. . . . He has not left himself without a witness in doing good—giving you rains from heaven and fruitful seasons, and filling you with food and your hearts with joy" (Acts 14:15, 17 NRSV). The Spirit's common grace can be observed in the lives of Melchizedek (Gen. 14), Abimelech (Gen. 20), and the sailors in Jonah's boat (Jonah 1).

Perhaps as strong a biblical rationale for the importance of common grace is that found within the pages of Ecclesiastes. But because of the difficulty interpreters have had in hearing both sides of its paradoxical argument (see appendix A), this message has often been missed (or dismissed as too little or too cynical or too secular or . . .). Thus, it is useful at the outset of this book to introduce Qoheleth's overall viewpoint, something that will prove advantageous for the chapters that follow as a variety of contemporary movies engage this biblical book in dialogue.[18]

Writing late in Israel's history (perhaps 350 B.C.), the writer of Ecclesiastes, Qoheleth, mounts a frontal attack on our misguided attempts to master life by pointing out life's limits and mysteries. Wisdom, according to the Book of Proverbs (1:5), involves the "art of steering"[19] (cf. the translation in the New Jerusalem Bible, "the art of guidance"). Wisdom helps one pilot oneself through the contradictions of life, much like a boat sailing down a fjord that contains rocks, both seen and submerged.

Observations easily morph into instructions, however. Once voiced, they can become absolutized, if not by the creators, then by the succeeding generations of followers. What begins as an art form—as the recording of observations on life—degenerates into cold calculation and hard work. Life's mystery and grace are in the process robbed of their charm.

The writer of Ecclesiastes seeks to set a limit on wisdom in this regard. Life is not a matter of hard work; its meaning does not open up before us like a problem being solved. Rather, wisdom is more like a flower blossoming forth into beauty. There is some order and regularity, but life's mystery and grace elude our grasp. Pluck it—remove it from the dirt—and death results.

As we have observed, some have found this Old Testament writer to be a pessimist, believing there is nothing of sure value in life. Others have thought him a cynic, believing there is no discernible meaning in life. I would disagree with both judgments, seeing the author as calling the wisdom tradition back to its central focus—the enjoyment of life from God. We cannot control life or nail it down. Life is simply too messy for that. Working to get riches (2:18–23; 4:7–8; 5:10–17), wisdom (1:16–18; 2:12–17), or pleasure (2:1–12) makes no sense to Qoheleth, for in the end, we all die (2:14–16; 3:19–20). Moreover, life too often proves amoral (6:1–6; 8:9–14), and its purposes remain mysterious (3:1–13). What we have done will be forgotten (1:11; 2:16; 4:16), and what is to be always remains unknowable (6:12; 7:14). Given life's reality, it is better not even to have been born (4:2; cf. 2:17). Yet life as God's gift should be enjoyed as we are enabled to do so (3:13; 9:7–10). This is our lot, or portion. "A live dog is better off than a dead lion" (9:4). We cannot save ourselves, but neither should we disparage life. Life may seem a contradiction, but that does not preclude our finding real joy in it. Qoheleth can, paradoxically, both decry and celebrate life's possibilities in the same breath.

As Elizabeth Huwiler points out in her perceptive commentary on Ecclesiastes, scholars have had difficulty giving equal emphasis to the book's negative evaluations and its positive call:

> A particular challenge for interpreters is the fact that Qohelet clings tenaciously to both claims: all life is *hebel,* and yet joy is both possible and good. It is important not to make one of these claims the only message of the book and dismiss the other as either a distraction or a grudging qualification. Qohelet insists on both, and often in the same passage. Thus any interpretation that attempts to separate them or exclude one is a distortion.[20]

Observable life lacks coherence, and yet the joys of common grace are also to be valued. We will all die, yet God gives us the days of our lives, the ability to eat and find enjoyment, our wealth and work, even our very spirit, or breath. Qoheleth challenges his readers to hold on to these two realities—*hebel* (vanity) and *simhah* (joy)—muting neither.

In an article I wrote on Ecclesiastes, I argued that we need to distinguish between the author's "intention" (his frontal assault on our misguided attempts to make life significant) and his "intentionality" (his mind-set or underlying consciousness, which recognizes that God's gifts in life are to be enjoyed).[21] Elsa Tamaz has recently argued similarly: "Qoheleth is clear: life is celebrated with gladness in the midst of enslaving labor, in the midst of *hebel* [vanity, uselessness, absurdity]." What Qoheleth proposes, she writes, "is to live today in the midst of the *hebel*, in the midst of the vanity, in the midst of the absurdity—but not according to it."[22]

Our Contemporary Cultural Context

Of course, biblical interpretation, like filmmaking, does not exist in a cultural vacuum. Basic to the increased willingness of both filmmakers and biblical exegetes to explore life's simultaneous meaningfulness and meaninglessness, to accept paradox and contradiction as an expression of life's messiness, is a change of mind-set that has been taking place in the larger, Western culture. Take, for example, the advice offered by New York's mayor Rudolph Giuliani during the Christmas season following 9/11. Interviewed on the television show *Extra,* he said, "I tell New Yorkers they have to learn how to mourn and cry, even while at the same time celebrating Christmas with more enthusiasm."[23]

The same paradox was present for Americans during the initial stages of the war with Iraq. During the Academy Awards, filmmakers struggled to determine the appropriate level of celebration given the conflict. A few stars canceled, feeling the event out of place. Ironically, the two most honored movies of the evening were *Chicago* and *The Pianist,* each embodying one or the other side of the contradiction. Celebration and pain were thus brought together. The NCAA basketball tournament was also televised during the conflict. In one of the early games, producers even juxtaposed the thrill of the game with updates of the war. The lines between sports and politics, entertainment and reality, were clear, and yet they were also blurred. Myles Brand, the president of the NCAA, justified the tournament in these words: "We're not going to let a tyrant determine how we're going to lead our lives." But others, such as Utah basketball coach Rick Majerus, were not so sure. Continuing to play in the tournament didn't feel right to him, given family members who had died in World War II, classmates who had died in Vietnam, and current soldiers whose families lived in his town.[24]

The comedian Jerry Lewis could say in the 1960s, "There are three things that are real to me—God, human folly, and laughter. Since the first two are beyond our comprehension, we must do what we can with the third."[25] This escapism worked in the 1950s and early 1960s. It was still "Camelot," a time of high idealism. But by the start of the new millennium, both God and human folly were demanding (and receiving) more airtime. During the Super Bowl telecast in January of 2001, the brokerage house Charles Schwab ran an ad. As we watched a young daughter being tucked into bed, we heard the unseen mother telling her a bedtime story about a prince sweeping her off her feet and taking her to his castle, where she was given everything she ever wanted. The camera then moved back to reveal the mother's identity: Sarah Ferguson! Fergie then quickly added, "Of course, if it doesn't work out, you need to know how to manage your stocks." The ad was clear, as was the underlying message. There are no fairy tales, just hard reality and the need to be able to fend for oneself. To attract clients, this ad used humor to give human folly a positive, albeit ironic, spin.

Providing an overview of the year's popular culture as 2002 came to a close, one newspaper critic found strange affinities between *Spider-Man,* Eminem, the Left Behind novels, Dr. Phil, and such video games as "Grand Theft Auto: Vice City." "Collectively," he wrote, "they represent a moment in time when America alternately [simultaneously] swaggered and trembled, flexed its muscles and murmured its prayers." The commentator quoted *Publishers Weekly* editor Nora Rawlinson: "My crackpot theory is that it has a lot to do with 9/11. The psyche of the country is one that wants stories that talk about grieving and death and [yet] give a positive spin on it."[26] As if to punctuate Rawlinson's remarks, the Academy Awards just three months later gave Pedro Almodovar an Oscar for best original screenplay. His script, *Hable Con Ella* (Talk to Her), put a positive spin on the developing friendship of two men who are both caring for a comatose lover. One finds joy in his beloved, despite her inability to respond in any way; the other finds joy through his new friend. Theirs is not just a denial of pain. Rather, in their pain, something wonder-filled is experienced.

In a privately circulated paper about American attitudes and beliefs at the turn of the millennium, J. Walker Smith, president of the market research firm Yankelovich Partners, outlined what he saw as an emerging "America.2." Central to his analysis was the belief that judgments are rooted today in the simultaneous "experience of good and bad in everything." He illustrated the culture's deep-seated sense of paradox by noting the polls concerning Bill Clinton. The former president's ratings as a good public servant remained high, even as his ratings as a private citizen were low. Clinton was not simply good or bad but both "good and bad at once."[27]

Two generations ago we still sought Camelot, believing that we could figure out what was unambiguously good and work to accomplish it. But such idealism was shattered by the assassinations of John F. Kennedy, Robert Kennedy, and Martin Luther King Jr., as well as by Vietnam. Money and smarts came to be seen as not necessarily enough to muscle aside limits or imperfections (though such thoughts still linger in some). Pessimism regarding the future became so dark that we called the next generation of children "X." Yet by the last decade of the twentieth century, according to Smith, many had "quit doing battle with paradox and made peace with it." Polls showed that we were "generally optimistic" while also being pessimistic about a growing number of things—Social Security, Medicare, crime, education, the budget, and so on. Life, it seems, was both much better than before and just as bad as always. As Smith noted, "Our optimism has not displaced nor relieved any of our apprehensions or fears. . . . Across the board, we expect to find good and bad joined together like Siamese twins, one always in the company of the other." What was the case in 1999, when Smith made these observations, has simply intensified in the years since, given 9/11, the decline of the stock market, and the war with Iraq.

According to Smith, what's smart now is to learn how "to live with and succeed by means of paradox." Absolutes seem naive. We have not lost our ability to distinguish good from bad, right from wrong, but any fundamentalism is self-defeating. It is better to be iconoclastic and ironic in treating traditional sources of authority and information, even while remaining hopeful nonetheless. We have become deeply suspicious of the church, for example, even as we open ourselves to the transcendent in other ways. Interest in spirituality has skyrocketed in American culture, whether it is spiritualism, faith healing, astrology, reincarnation, mysticism, or even voodoo. But suspicion of the church has also increased—case in point, the fallout from Cardinal Law's stonewalling of child abuse charges in the Boston archdiocese. Volvo tried to capitalize on such contradiction with an ad that parodied it: "Our most impressive safety innovation yet. A Volvo that can save your soul." MasterCard was perhaps even savvier with its campaign, which focused on getting our priorities straight: "There are some things money can't buy. For everything else, there's MasterCard." What these marketers realized is that in the postmodern world the quest for material well-being and the pursuit of spiritual satisfaction can proceed simultaneously.

"Paradox," suggested Smith, "is the new chic." Contradiction, its outward expression, is thus being celebrated today in numerous ways. In fashion, for example, retroeclectic is in. So too is the mixing of Tommy and Target. In television, *Politically Incorrect* brought together disparate people from such fields as religion, politics, entertainment, and education to provide contradictory opinions and ironic banter about current events. The show often expressed not only outrage over what was happening but also the outrageous. The show was pulled after Bill Maher, the host, proved to be too controversial for his network when he criticized the American lifestyle as contributing to 9/11, but his cultural instincts were sound.

Life's Paradox

What has popularly been labeled the move from late modernity to postmodernity in Western culture has brought with it fundamental changes in how we view reality. Rather than witnessing efforts either to engineer life or to bemoan life's futility, culture has seen a new kind of wisdom emerge—one centered in paradox and contradiction. This new savvy is not first of all abstract theory; it arises from lived experience. (Here is the helpful distinction between postmodernism, a philosophical system, and postmodernity, life as it is expressed in the twenty-first century.) Rationality is not enough if we are to know life; the whole person must be engaged. As any viewer of the *X-Files* knows, we must have not only Scully (reason) but also Mulder (faith), and vice versa. Again, a simple pragmatism will not do. What Prudential advertised for decades, "Own a piece of the rock," has given way to "Be your own rock." Saab's billboards urge, "Find your own road." But while self-directed, such savvy should not be mistaken for mere self-reliance.[28] Attempts to go it alone have little chance of success in our complex world. What the new smarts is about is empowerment, not individual competence or abstract theory. Wisdom is rooted in the experience of paradox and results in a battered optimism, a commitment to a useless beauty that is transformative.

The chapters that follow explore the contours of "all this useless beauty," both by reflecting on selected contemporary movies and by placing them in dialogue with the Book of Ecclesiastes. Having put on cinematic spectacles to see anew ancient truth, we will return in the final chapter to consider again the wisdom of this Old Testament sage, hoping to see *(ra'ah)* how better to steer ourselves through life's shoals.

In his book *How Can It Be All Right When Everything Is All Wrong?* the late Lewis Smedes wrote what can serve both as a summary for this chapter and as an invitation to read further:

Joy also has to be compatible with the pain within me. To promise joy without pain is Pollyannaism, make-believe, deceit. Legitimate joy must be the experience of joy along with pain. And it seems to me possible. Maybe there is more joy in Watts than in Palm Springs. Maybe joy is more real lodged in the interstices of pain than as the climax of a pleasure trip. Maybe joy in this life always has to be "in spite" of something. The joy of a person with an inoperable brain tumor can be infinitely deeper than the thrill of a birdie on the eighteenth hole.[29]

2

THE EXISTENTIALIST ALTERNATIVE

Akira Kurosawa and Woody Allen

> The spirit of the Preacher is strong today in our minds. His mood fills our philosophy and poetry. The vanity of human existence is described powerfully by those who call themselves philosophers or poets of existence. They are all children of the Preacher, the great existentialist of his period.
>
> Paul Tillich, *The New Being* (1955)

The correlation between cultural and philosophical shifts and changes in biblical interpretation has often been noted. Galileo's recognition that the earth moved around the sun, and not vice versa, brought with it changes in how we read the biblical text (e.g., "the sun stood still" [Josh. 10:13]). A new cosmology created the need for a new figurative interpretation, lest Scripture's authority be undermined. Similarly, the Enlightenment brought a new historiography and the need to understand biblical history and chronology in a new light. A historical-critical paradigm for interpreting the biblical text was the result. Social unrest in Latin America gave rise to liberation theology and a biblical hermeneutic developed from the underside, one with the eyes of the poor. In analogous ways, the rise of existentialism as a dominant philosophical force following World War II created an occasion to reinterpret biblical texts in its light. Nowhere was this seen more clearly than in the existentialist interpretation of the Book of Ecclesiastes.

Existentialism's roots can be traced to the nineteenth century with its twin towers of reason and progress. What if my world is not always reasonable, and what if human progress is for me a lie? The existential revolt began with such questioning by several lonely, eccentric thinkers and artists whose lives were characterized by suffering. They included Søren Kierkegaard (1813–55), Fyodor Dostoyevsky (1821–81), Vincent van Gogh (1853–90), and Friedrich Nietzsche (1844–1900). Some of these prophets directed their cries to a God who seemed hidden *(Deus absconditus);* others turned away, believing there was no God at all. This religious divide continues in the present, but what Kierkegaard found true for himself is characteristic of the beginning point for all: We are all alone in the silence of a strange world:

> One sticks one's finger into the soil to tell by the smell in what land one is: I stick my finger into existence—it smells of nothing. Where am I? Who am I? How came I here? What is this thing called the world? . . . How did I come into the world? Why was I not consulted . . . but was thrust into the ranks? . . . How did I obtain an interest in this big enterprise they call reality? Why should I have an interest in it? Is it a voluntary concern? And if I am compelled to take part in it, where is the director?[1]

Such questioning took on a new urgency with the outbreak of World War I. Neither reason nor progress seemed inevitable. Poets such as T. S. Eliot and Ezra Pound, novelists such as Franz Kafka and James Joyce, playwrights Eugene O'Neill and Bertolt Brecht, artists such as Picasso and Giacometti, musicians Arnold Schoen-

berg and Anton Webern, even physicists such as Werner Heisen-
berg and Niels Bohr all questioned previous notions of coherence,
rationality, and order, as well as humankind's ability to "know" or
to "do." The world seemed dissonant and/or irrational, and what
was exposed was humankind's vulnerability and nakedness in the
face of it. The Great Depression, Hitler's genocide of the Jews, and
the atomic bomb only added to the homelessness of the human
spirit. The world seemed, in a word, absurd.

Thus, with the ending of World War II's hostilities, existentialism
broke on to the world scene as part of the furniture of modern life.
Chief among its interpreters were Jean-Paul Sartre and Albert Camus.
Though no summary can adequately deal with existentialism's bewil-
dering range of thought, which by definition was individualistic and
often contradictory, a general shape can be recognized: (1) The world
is inexplicable and absurd. As residents in it, we sense the homelessness
of our human spirit. (2) This raises the question, What does it mean
to be a human? And how can we search out and value that humanity, once discovered? (3) Such questions are not abstract reflections.
Rather, they are the passionate, individual cries of human beings,
cries that move us out into the world. Truth, in short, is earned only
by experience. And it is "my truth" that matters. (4) Moreover, we
experience what it means to be human "on the boundary." It is only
"the real 'bite of experience' . . . the deep things of personal experience
which make us know—through love and sorrow, through nostalgia
and joy, through death and loss—that a man's life is not any sort of
intellectual puzzle to be ferreted out but a gift to be received and a
task to be fulfilled."[2]

Here is an approach to truth. It begins with the question, Who
am I in this absurd world moving toward death? It is not surprising
that some biblical scholars found such a question akin to what is
asked in Ecclesiastes, where the theme of life's futility runs from beginning to end. "Vanity of vanities, says the Teacher, vanity of vanities!
All is vanity" (1:2 NRSV). "Vanity of vanities, says the Teacher; all is
vanity" (12:8 NRSV). Moreover, Qoheleth responds to life's absurdity
in radically personal terms. His short book is written largely in the
first person. He says that in his vain life, "*I* have seen everything"
(7:15, emphasis added). Over and over (forty-six times in this short

book) we read of what he saw. Sometimes his "seeing" has the sense of "to know," other times "to observe," "to discern," "to look into," or "to perceive." But always, we are being let into his own personal, passionate search for life's meaning. Qoheleth committed himself to "examine and study all the things that are done in this world" (1:13), and when he did, he discovered that "it is all useless. . . . You can't straighten out what is crooked" (1:14–15). Life thus "came to mean nothing to me. . . . I had been chasing the wind" (2:17).

As with the existentialists, existence seemed to lack both rationality and meaning for Qoheleth; though he wanted to know, he couldn't find out. Michael Fox, perhaps the best-known scholar of Ecclesiastes who sees the book in existential terms, states:

> Qohelet does not have a way to say "meaningful," but he does have its antonym, absurd. To express this, he makes metaphorical use of the word *hebel* [which Fox translates as "absurd"]. . . . The essence of "absurd" is, as Camus says, *contradiction*. Thus the absurd is irrational, an affront to reason."[3]

We have already noted Qoheleth's commitment to contradiction. Toil is without profit, yet we are to enjoy it. Wisdom is valuable, yet it also reveals life's bitterness and is vulnerable to folly. Life is at times arbitrary and unjust, even if God is just. Life is precious, yet death cancels out everything. "All life is *hebel;* and yet joy is both possible and good."[4]

Like Sisyphus, Qoheleth has a compulsion for knowledge that cannot be fully met. "What he is lamenting," in Fox's words, "is the refractory, paradoxical, cussed quality of reality. Significance cannot be *read* out of events."[5] Nevertheless, thinks Fox, Qoheleth's nobility comes in his effort, as he pushes the border of wisdom's limitation.[6]

Despite clear similarities, however, the question must be raised, Is such an existentialist understanding of life compatible with that of Qoheleth? In particular, even if the "diagnosis" of our ills is similar, is the proposed "cure" the same? Or does a subtle misreading of the text intrude? It is difficult to answer such a question abstractly. As existentialism has recognized, knowledge follows experience; it does not precede it. In the modern era following World War II and extending into the 1990s, filmmakers enfleshed their existential questions and answers in stories, thus providing "examples" that breathed with life. Two of the best of these were Akira Kurosawa and Woody Allen. In turning to their portrayals of life on the boundary, we can hope to arrive at a better understanding not only of existentialism's similarities but also of its differences with regard to the wisdom of the Old Testament sage. We can also observe a contrast with the wisdom emerging from a younger generation of Hollywood filmmakers.

Akira Kurosawa

> To be an artist means never to avert one's eyes.
>
> Akira Kurosawa[7]

Akira Kurosawa, the Japanese director and screenwriter, made thirty films over fifty-five years before dying in 1998 at the age of eighty-eight. One of the giants of the cinema, he influenced filmmaking worldwide as few others have.* Steven Spielberg considered him "the pictorial Shakespeare of our time." Martin Scorcese spoke of his "Passion. Dynamism. Force. Exhilaration. Speed. Terrible Beauty." Francis Ford Coppola thought he should be the first filmmaker to be awarded a Nobel Prize.[8] The Academy of Motion Picture Arts and Sciences in 1989 presented him with an honorary Academy Award "for accomplishments that have inspired, delighted, enriched, and entertained audiences and influenced filmmakers throughout the world."[9] Kurosawa was a humanist who through his existential depic-

---

*Several of Kurosawa's movies were remade for Hollywood. *The Seven Samurai* (1954) became *The Magnificent Seven; Rashomon* (1950) put Japanese film on the map, and its premise was later reworked in *Courage under Fire* (d. Zwick, 1996). Anyone who has seen George Lucas's *Star Wars* knows the plot of *The Hidden Fortress* (1958). And not only did *Yojimbo* (1961) become the "spaghetti Western," *A Fistful of Dollars* staring Clint Eastwood, but its lead character has inspired a host of other stoic antiheroes: Mel Gibson in *Mad Max*, Bruce Willis in *Pulp Fiction*, Arnold Schwarzenegger in *Terminator 2*, and both Charles Bronson and Clint Eastwood in almost every film they have been in.

tion of life fought to retain a sense of hope in a world he perceived to have become meaningless in the midst of great social change.

A master of the two most popular kinds of Japanese movies during his era, the *jidai-geki* (the costumed samarai films set in medieval times) and the *gendai-geki* (the realistic, domestic dramas set in contemporary Japanese life), Kurosawa anchored his movies in the Japanese culture and spirit. Nevertheless, Japanese critics thought him "too Western," for in giving shape to his stories, Kurosawa often borrowed from Western literary sources (Tolstoy, Shakespeare, Goethe, Dostoyevsky). Kurosawa rejected such criticism, saying, "I collect old Japanese lacquerware as well as antique French and Dutch glassware."[10] Rather than being Eastern or Western, his films possess a universality that is rooted in what one of his literary mentors, Dostoyevsky, called "the 'eternal questions'—those of humans in their relations to themselves, their society, and their universe."[11]

Kurosawa's existential perception of life remained a constant throughout his body of films. His characters are typically on a personal quest for justice, rebelling against unresponsive social structures. Recognizing the apparent meaninglessness of their lives, particularly as they face the existential crisis of death, they have a compassion for those who suffer that sets them apart, as does their action in addressing an uncaring and indifferent world. In this way, his characters choose life, finding personal meaning if not social success.

In his last movie, *Madadayo* (Japanese release, 1993; USA release, 2000), Kurosawa tells the story of a Japanese *sensei*, a teacher, revered for his wisdom and humor, who loses everything in the bombings of World War II. Living in a cramped hut on a burned-out estate, he nevertheless celebrates his life with his adoring students at a yearly anniversary dinner. Kurosawa said, "The characters in my films try to live honestly and make the most of the lives they've been given. I believe you must live honestly and develop your abilities to the full. People who do this are the real heroes."[12] And such is this old *sensei*. Each year, the students offer tributes and songs to their professor-hero, followed by the chant *"Mahda-Kai?"* ("Are you ready yet?"). The *sensei* responds, *"Madadayo"* ("Not yet")—*madadayo* to death, sickness, disgrace, and all that would undercut his ability to say yes to life. The students then cheer as he downs a huge glass of beer. The movie *Madadayo* is slight—a simple portrait of a man full of grace and admired by his students who refuses to give in to circumstance or death, given his love of life. It is also extraordinarily moving, causing its viewers to consider their own need to shout *"madadayo."*

Ikiru

Living in the midst of chaotic times, Kurosawa believed we all must choose for ourselves a course of action. And in that choice, we have the opportunity to find life. Such an existential posture is nowhere clearer than in his movie *Ikiru* (1952). Written, directed, and edited by the master himself, *Ikiru* (To Live) is perhaps his most personal work. Achingly beautiful and often included in listings of the top one hundred films of all time, it tells the story of Kanji Watanabe (Takashi Shimura), a joyless, dying bureaucrat who, when faced with death, discovers a reason to live.

Told by an omniscient narrator who functions something like the *benshi* of silent Japanese cinema who both narrated and interpreted the events on the screen for the house audience, Watanabe's story is given, in this way, a purpose and a meaning beyond the simple act of storytelling. The movie's strong point of view has an indirect poignancy as well, for Kurosawa's closest brother, who introduced him to the cinema and was himself a *benshi*, committed suicide at age twenty-seven after sound movies made his job obsolete. Given a cold and harsh universe, how then is one "to live"?

The movie begins with the black-and-white image of an X-ray and the narrator's voice-over: "This is an X-ray picture of a stomach; it belongs to the man this story is about. Symptoms of cancer are there, but he doesn't yet know anything about it." Watanabe discovers his fate only indirectly as doctors, trying to hide the fact that he has but six months to live, use the same evasive language that a waiting room patient has told him would mean he has cancer. Denied by his doctor's cowardice even one individual to share his grief, Watanabe walks out of the hospital alone. The audience feels his pain as the sound track goes mute, and we are pulled into his world. Only when the noise of traffic suddenly erupts and the camera pulls back to reveal street traffic with a truck racing by him (and us!) do we realize that we have

Kanji Watanabe (Takashi Shimura), a city hall bureaucrat, must come to terms with his terminal cancer. *Ikiru* (d. Kurosawa, 1952). A Toho Production. Photofest. All rights reserved.

for that instant been suspended with Watanabe in his grief. *"We must all die—wise and foolish alike" (2:16).*

First given a picture of the dying man from the "inside," viewers are quickly shown Watanabe's deathlike existence on the "outside." He has worked at the Tokyo City Hall for thirty years, accomplishing little more than frustrating the desires of citizens who come to his desk asking for help. As the narrator says, "He's not very interesting yet. He's just passing the time, wasting it, rather. It would be difficult to say that he is really alive." In this way, the viewer is set up for what the story will be about: the movement from "death in life" to "life, given his impending death." *"It is better to go to a home where there is mourning than to one where there is a party, because the living should always remind themselves that death is waiting for us all" (7:2).* Qoheleth's truth eventually becomes Watanabe's as well, but, just as with the ancient sage, the redemptive possibilities that death provides are not immediately apparent to him.

Watanabe must first confront the absurdity of his present life. When Toyo, the only female office worker in his section, is reprimanded for laughing at a joke in a magazine and is forced to read it aloud, she reluctantly does:

"You've never had a day off, have you?"

"No."

"Why? Are you indispensable?"

"No. I don't want them to find out that they can do without me."

The camera slowly scans the faces of the work team sitting at the long table with Toyo. It begins and ends with Watanabe himself.

Watanabe comes to realize that he is the man Toyo describes. *"Only someone too stupid to find his way home would wear himself out with work" (10:15)*. Though he has never taken a day off, he is doing little, the narrator tells us. "He is like a corpse, and actually he has been dead for the past twenty-five years." *"You work and worry your way through life, and what do you have to show for it? As long as you live, everything you do brings nothing but worry and heartache. Even at night your mind can't rest. It is all useless" (2:22–23)*.

The meaninglessness of Watanabe's work is masterfully presented in a sequence showing housewives from the neighborhood appealing to him to have a park built on a small piece of swamp. But Watanabe is deaf to their request. Seen being shunted from one department to the next in a series of still shots linked by wipes, the women encounter department head after department head who speak to the camera as if they were addressing the citizens. Finally, the women have completed a circle, and they are back to Watanabe's station, where it all began. (These same department heads stonewall a new group of citizens as the movie ends.) *"Generations come and generations go, but the world stays just the same. . . . What has happened before will happen again. What has been done before will be done again. There is nothing new in the whole world" (1:4, 9)*.

It is not just work that is meaningless; Watanabe's family is also unable to provide consolation. Watanabe has worked to provide for his only son, but his son and daughter-in-law, with whom he lives, are selfish and ungrateful. In a series of perfectly executed dissolves that flip almost seamlessly between Watanabe's lonely present and his remembrances of times past, we see him calling for his son while flashbacks of his wife's funeral, a discussion of his possible remarriage, his son's mistake in a baseball game, his son's appendicitis, and his son going off to war are shown on the screen.* Death, error, illness, separation—life's past intrusions seem more significant than any present relationship. Watanabe pulls the covers over his head and weeps. *"You work for something with all your wisdom, knowledge, and skill, and then you have to leave it all to someone who hasn't had to work for it" (2:21).*

Watanabe realizes that he is alone, but for that reason he is also free to decide what he will do. At first, wanting simply to escape ("Eat, drink, and be merry, for tomorrow we die"), he gets drunk on expensive sake. It is "a protest against my life up to now," he tells a writer who befriends him at a bar. Watanabe continues, "I'd thought of ending it all, but it's hard to die. And I can't die just yet. I don't know what I've been living for all these years."

Given the meaninglessness of work and the absence of a loving family, Watanabe begins his search for life. With half of his life savings in his pocket, he asks his writer "friend" to show him a good time. The writer agrees to help him start "to live," saying he will be Watanabe's "Mephistopheles, but a good one, who won't ask to be paid."† In a frenzied night on the town, a cross section of modern Japan's vices—alcohol, pinball, dance clubs, a strip club—are tried and found wanting. At a cabaret, Watanabe is asked by the piano player if he has any favorites, and Watanabe recalls a haunting love song from the 1920s that he proceeds to sing:

> Life is so short,
> Fall in love, dear maiden,
> While your lips are still red,

---

*This sequence is a particularly brilliant piece of filmmaking. Watanabe sits down in the present exactly as he sits down in the past at the baseball game.

†Kurosawa told his co-screenwriter, Hideo Oguni, when he invited him to cowrite the script for *Ikiru*, that he "wanted to use Tolstoy's *The Death of Ivan Ilyich* as its basis" (Hideo Oguni, quoted in Stuart Galbraith IV, *The Emperor and the Wolf* [New York: Faber & Faber, 2001], 156). There is also a direct reference in the movie to Goethe's *Faust*, and scholars have noted the structural similarities between these two works.

Before you can no longer love—
For there will be no tomorrow.

Life is so short,
Fall in love, dear maiden,
While your hair is still black,
Before your heart stops—
For there will be no more tomorrow.

Watanabe's fellow revelers are stunned into silence as tears again stream down his face. *"Sorrow is better than laughter; it may sadden your face, but it sharpens your understanding. Someone who is always thinking about happiness is a fool. A wise person thinks about death. . . . When a fool laughs, it is like thorns crackling in a fire. It doesn't mean a thing"* (7:3–4, 6).

Next, Watanabe befriends Toyo. Her youthful exuberance is captivating. As he devotes himself to her, friends and family suspect Watanabe is having an affair, but such is not the case. Rather, he is, in his melancholy, seeking to exist through her. When the young woman confides to Watanabe that she has given everyone at the office a nickname and that his is "the Mummy," he is not offended. Longing for the passion of her youth, he tells her, "Just to look at you makes me feel better. It warms this—this mummy's heart of mine. . . . You're so full of life. And me . . . I'm jealous of that. If I could be like you for just one day before I died. I won't be able to die unless I can do that." *"So remember your Creator while you are still young, before those dismal days and years come when you will say, 'I don't enjoy life'"* (12:1).

Toyo, however, is increasingly uncomfortable with her relationship with the old man, as he buys her gifts and takes her out at night. It seems one-sided and unnatural. Repeating much of what he has told her earlier, Watanabe pleads, "If only I could be like you for one day before I die. I won't be able to die unless I can be. Oh, I want to *do* something. Only you can show me. I don't know what to *do*. I don't know how to *do* it." Toyo is perplexed. She has no advice to give: "But all I *do* is work and eat—that's all. . . . That and make toys like this one [she sets a wind-up rabbit on the table, and it hops toward him]. That's all I *do,* but it's fun. I feel as if I were friends with all the children in Japan now. Mr. Watanabe, why don't you *do* something like that too?" Here is the answer Watanabe has been seeking—something he can hold on to as he is drowning: "I can *do* something if I really want to!" he exclaims (emphasis added).

Watanabe picks up the rabbit and hurries down the stairs to the strains of the song boys and girls are singing at a party behind him, "Happy birthday to you, happy birthday to you!" It is Watanabe's birthday too; he has been reborn. Watanabe is quickly shown back at his office rummaging through his desk looking for something. It is the housewives' petition to reclaim the drainage area and make it a park in their neighborhood. He will get the park built and sets about his task. This is the last time we see him alive. *"The end of something is better than its beginning" (7:8).*

The stark X-ray that opened the movie has dominated the narration up to this moment. Watanabe's life has been marked by death, both literally and figuratively. Now, in the final third of the movie, we see in a series of flashbacks how Watanabe discovered life, given death. The narrator announces that it is five months later and Watanabe has died. By having his death come in this way, in the middle of the story, we as viewers are able to center our attention on the meaning of Watanabe's life, not on his impending but inevitable death.

The scene shifts to the wake, which is at Watanabe's house. Though we have seldom seen Watanabe at his house in the film, we come to understand that he is, at last, "at home." His fellow government office workers are present with his family. Little by little we are let in on the story as his colleagues ask one another what happened. Why did he change? Did he know he was dying? Not always themselves understanding the significance of what they recall, his colleagues drink themselves drunk, telling their stories. On the screen, brief flashbacks allow viewers to slowly piece together the significance of Watanabe's deed.

At first Watanabe's coworkers and superiors are convinced that they were responsible for the park being built, even as the press and the women petitioners who arrive at the wake counter their comments. But Watanabe's singular resolve soon becomes evident amid the vacuity of his colleagues' bureaucratic life. "I don't know what it was that was keeping Mr. Watanabe alive," observed one coworker. "When he looked at the park . . . his face just glowed. It was . . . well, it was like a man looking at his own grandchild," said another. "In this organization where you can't *do* anything, Mr. Watanabe *did* something, and he *did* it because he had cancer," offers a third. Fighting both indifference and intimidation, Watanabe chose to act; he willed a park into being.

Finally, a policeman arrives and admits that he saw Watanabe in the park the night he died. He is remorseful because he did not intervene, thinking Watanabe simply drunk. But Watanabe's joy came from another source. He chose and accomplished his life's mission. In a flashback, we see Watanabe sitting on a swing, singing the same love song from his youth that he had sung earlier. But this time as he sings the haunting song, he is happy, serene. There are no tears flowing down his face, even as he awaits his death. "Life is so short, / Fall in love, dear maiden, / While your lips are still red, / Before you can no longer love— / For there will be no tomorrow." *"Young people, enjoy your youth. Be happy while you are still young . . . before those dismal days . . . when the light of the sun . . . will grow dim for you . . . your arms, that have protected you, will tremble, and your legs, now strong, will grow weak . . . and all desire will have gone"* (11:9; 12:1–3, 5).

It is not ultimately Watanabe's courage given his cancer or even his activity in having the park built but rather his resultant joy in living that is to be celebrated. To the bleak reportage that characterizes the first two-thirds of the movie Kurosawa adds sublime, visual poetry. *"Here is what I have found out: the best thing we can do is . . . enjoy what we have worked for during the short life that God has given us; this is our fate"* (5:18). Such enjoyment might not seem like much, but it is everything.

Existentialism, Ecclesiastes, and Ikiru

Ikiru, like its Old Testament counterpart, thus has two foci. The one is a biting indictment of the social system that has produced a widespread "cancer" among its citizens. The second concerns the discovery of personal meaning and joy that are possible as we choose to act for the benefit of others. And the link between the two stories is the X-ray—in death is found life.

In both *Ikiru* and Ecclesiastes, the same meaningless situation is recognized (life's absurdity, chief of which is death itself), and many of the same false solutions are attempted (work, pleasure). But when Kurosawa turns to portray what it is to live, his existential answer misses the spirit of the Old Testament sage. It has too much to do with "doing" rather than with "being."

Critics are nearly unanimous in finding in *Ikiru* strong existential themes. Living amid absurdity, we must choose a course of action. In the process, we find meaning. Donald Richie, Kurosawa's foremost interpreter, begins his introduction to the printed film script by quoting Richard Brown with approval:

> Akira Kurosawa's *Ikiru* is a cinematic expression of modern existential thought. It consists of a restrained affirmation within the context of a giant negation. What it says in starkly lucid terms is that "life" is meaningless. At the same time, one man's life can acquire meaning when he undertakes to perform some task, which *to him* is meaningful. What anyone else thinks about that man's life is beside the point, even ludicrous. The meaning of his life is what he commits the meaning of his life to be. There is nothing else.[13]

Richie believes that as with Dostoyevsky's Myushikin, Sartre's Roquetin, and Camus's Rambert, "Watanabe discovers himself through 'doing.'"[14] After layer on layer is peeled away and Watanabe stands alone, responsible for himself, his choice to act constitutes his person. The park was only "a pretext for this action," believes Richie.[15]

David Desser makes a helpful correction to Richie's comments when he notes that *Ikiru* actually takes up two thematic questions: "the problem of life's meaning in an existential, absurd world" and that of "ordinary heroism."[16] In Kurosawa's world, action alone, irrespective of ethical intention or outcome, is insufficient to define an individual. Desser summarizes, "Surely the kind of action taken is crucial to our appreciation of Watanabe, and to Kurosawa's view of man as an ethical being, as one who must choose to act rightly in the face of absurdity. That is what heroism means; that is what it means to live."[17] The point of Toyo making toy rabbits ("I feel as if I were friends with all the children in Japan now") and of Watanabe building the park ("unless we do something about it, nothing will ever be done") is accomplishing something for others, even in the face of absurdity.

But whether involving pure action (Richie) or purposeful action (Desser), Kurosawa's understanding of how we might cope existentially in a meaningless world means creating by our own effort our own meaning. As such, it is far from Qoheleth's view. In Ecclesiastes, meaning is unknowable, except as it is discovered as a gift from our Creator. Kurosawa's existential answer to our being thrown alone into the world has more to do with "task" (in German, *Aufgabe*) than with "gift" (in German, *Gabe*). We are, believes Kurosawa, to create our own meaning by the choices we make. Contrast this with Qoheleth's advice: *"The best thing we can do is eat and drink and enjoy what we have worked for during the short life that God has given us. . . . Since God has allowed us to be happy, we will not worry too much about how short life is" (5:18, 20).*

Woody Allen

> Existential subjects to me are still the only subjects worth dealing with.
>
> Woody Allen[18]

> I think that at best the universe is indifferent. At best!
>
> Woody Allen[19]

In his movie *Crimes and Misdemeanors* (1989), Woody Allen offers perhaps his most telling portrayal of the human condition. He provides his viewers two takes on human existence—the "real" and the "reel." The film, which Allen both wrote and directed, shows two parallel stories that intersect only in the last ten minutes, when the chief characters come together at a wedding. In one storyline, Cliff Stern (Woody Allen), a second-rate filmmaker trapped in a sterile marriage, falls in love with Halley Reed (Mia Farrow), an attractive

PBS producer, only to lose her to his brother-in-law Lester (Alan Alda), a self-important but successful filmmaker. Cliff is making a documentary on the hopeful and courageous philosophy of the existentialist Louis Levy (Martin Bergmann), that is, until Levy's suicide! Cliff's best friend is his young niece Jenny (Jenny Nichols), whom he enjoys taking to the movies. In fact, Hollywood's "reels" provide him his only solace.

The second storyline revolves around Judah Rosenthal (Martin Landau), a successful ophthalmologist who has exchanged his father's religious wisdom ("the eyes of God are on us always") for secular, medical knowledge. He is trying to end a two-year affair with Dolores Paley (Anjelica Huston), who is threatening to expose him. Facing up to his need to silence her, Judah has his underworld brother, Jack (Jerry Orbach), hire an anonymous hit man to kill her. By doing so, he rejects the alternate advice of his patient, the rabbi Ben (Sam Waterston), Cliff's brother-in-law, who believes there is "a moral structure to the universe" and wants Judah to confess to his wife and ask for forgiveness.

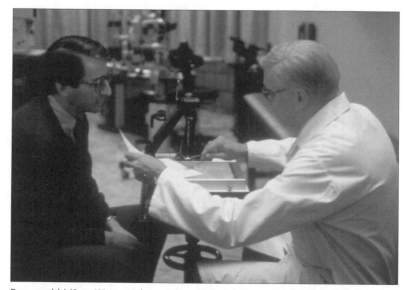

Ben, a rabbi (Sam Waterston), consults with Judah Rosenthal (Martin Landau), a successful ophthalmologist, about his failing eyesight. *Crimes and Misdemeanors* (d. Allen, 1989). Photo by Brian Hamill.

As these complicated plots unfold, Allen cuts back and forth sharply between the stories. The movie in this way resembles a novel more than a typical movie. But the juxtaposition of these two stories—Cliff's comic "misdemeanors," which are set to jazz, and Judah's dark "crimes," whose musical background is Schubert—allows Allen to explore the universal existential themes that have fascinated him throughout his professional career.

The moral core of the movie can be seen particularly in two scenes. The first is a Seder that Judah reconstructs in his mind as he stands in the doorway of the dining room in the home in which he grew up. His father, Sol, a conservative Jew, is having an argument with his skeptical aunt May. She is telling her brother, "Don't fill their heads with superstition." "Might makes right." "Do you challenge the whole moral impulse?" asks another at the table. "For those who want morality, there's morality. Nothing's handed down in stone," is her reply. When the adult Judah intrudes into his reverie to ask, "If a man commits a crime, if he . . . if he kills . . ." His father responds that a man who murders will be punished. Judah is shocked to hear the word *murder* being used, but his aunt May eases his guilt by her retort, "And I say, if he can do it and get away with it, and he chooses not to be bothered by the ethics, then he's home free." Finally, when pushed to make a choice, his father blurts out, "If necessary, I will always choose God over truth." But for the viewer, neither Aunt May's *Realpolitik* nor Sol's *sacrificum intellectus* is satisfactory. Here is the dilemma.

In *Crimes and Misdemeanors,* there are those, like the rabbi Ben, who choose religious meaning over truth, but they are portrayed as blind. There are those, like Professor Levy, who propose love as an answer to a hostile and barren world but commit suicide. And there are the artists, filmmakers like Lester and Cliff, who are either ineffectual or self-serving. Anchoring life's meaning in religion, philosophy, or art proves inadequate to life's reality. They are pseudo-realities. But can we instead embrace "might makes right"?

The second scene shows Ben, who is now blind, hosting the reception for his daughter and her new husband. Judah and Cliff are both among the guests. In an ironic reversal of the "reel" and the "real," Judah tells Cliff that he has "a great murder story. Great plot." He then proceeds to tell Cliff as if it were fiction the real-life story of his murder of Dolores. He concludes the story by saying that the man suffered weeks of guilt, for "suddenly it's not an empty universe at all, but a just and moral one." Eventually, however, the man's guilt and obsession with his father's God passes, and rather than being punished, he actually prospers. "His life is completely back to normal, back to his protected world of wealth and privilege. . . . Oh, maybe once in a while he has a bad moment, but it passes. With time it all fades."

Cliff is horrified with what he has heard.

> Cliff: I would have him turn himself in, 'cause then you see, then your story assumes tragic proportions, because in the absence of a God or something he is forced to assume that responsibility himself. Then you have tragedy.

> Judah: But that's fiction; that's movies. You see too many movies. I'm talking about reality. I mean if you want a happy ending, you should go see a Hollywood movie.

Morality and religion may serve as the foundation for great literature, but their attempts at producing a happy ending line up poorly with reality. It is better, thinks Judah, to face existence head-on, doing what must be done to carve out a meaningful life. As the scene ends, Judah and his wife leave the party hand in hand, talking of the wedding reception they will be throwing for their daughter. But is this to be believed? Could Judah's they-lived-happily-ever-after reality really be a model to live by?

To help his viewers remain focused on how best to "see" life, Allen makes constant use of (at times overuse of) the metaphor of sight. Judah is an ophthalmologist; Ben becomes blind; Sol is told by his sister to open his eyes; Cliff and Lester see life through their camera lens; Dolores speaks of the eyes as "the windows of the soul," and after she is murdered, Judah tells his brother, "There was nothing behind her eyes. All you saw was a black void." Allen extends the visual metaphor by juxtaposing film clips with real life, providing in the process ironic commentary on how events might be seen.

After watching Judah try to convince Dolores to end their affair, for example, the movie cuts to Cliff and Jenny, who are watching Hitchcock's *Mr. and Mrs. Smith*. Carole Lombard is complaining that Robert Montgomery wants to "throw me aside like a squeezed lemon." And in perhaps the funniest moment of the film, Cliff shows Lester the documentary Lester has commissioned Cliff to make of him. Lester is aghast as he is compared visually to both a talking mule and Mussolini. He yells, "The idea was to show the real me!" Viewers are in this way asked to decide who is the real Lester.

On the surface, as Mark Roche observes, "Allen opts more for the sight of the ophthalmologist Judah (who sees superficial reality clearly) than the inner vision of the rabbi (who offers an ideal to counter reality)."[20] Ben is, after all, blind to the real world, both literally and figuratively. But as the movie ends, Ben is seen joyously dancing with his daughter at her wedding. He is in love with life—with his family and his faith. Allen, himself, has observed:

> Ben is . . . blind even before he goes blind. He's blind because he doesn't see the real world. But he's blessed and lucky because he has the single most important attribute anyone could have, the best gift anyone could have. He has genuine religious faith. . . . And so even in the face of the worst adversity, he is OK. He goes blind. He still loves life and loves his daughter. . . . But as the author, I think that Ben is blind even before he's blind, because he doesn't see what's real in the world. But he's lucky, because he has his naiveté.[21]

There is a similarly structured tension in the character of Judah. Given the angst that he exhibits even as he narrates his great plot, his "Hollywood" ending has yet to be fully tested by reality. Will he really move on so blithely? Judah is lucky because he has emerged scot-free. But he has also been reminded that he is a murderer.

As the movie ends, this intended ambiguity concerning life and its meaning is reinforced by a concluding voice-over, heard while flashbacks of previous scenes are shown. The voice is that of Professor Levy:

We are in fact the sum total of our choices. Events unfold so unpredictably, so unfairly, human happiness does not seem to have been included in the design of creation. It is only we, with our capacity to love, that give meaning to the indifferent universe. And yet most human beings seem to have the ability to keep trying, and even to find joy from simple things, like their family, their work, and from the hope that future generations might understand more.

The irony, of course, is that Levy also penned the words "I went out the window" just before committing suicide. Can any of his other words have any significance? Allen deconstructs Levy's existentialist hope further through a montage of images that foreground his concluding voice-over. We see not only Ben dancing joyously with his daughter but also Dolores and Judah arguing, Cliff kissing Halley (who in the end has chosen Lester), and Judah hearing from Jack that the murder has been accomplished. Life is messy. It has an ambiguity and a moral uncertainty that cannot be escaped, thinks Allen. Judah gets away with murder; Levy commits suicide; Ben goes blind; Cliff retreats into fantasy; and Lester is a pompous fool. We live in an empty and unfriendly world. As with the writer of Ecclesiastes, we must conclude that life is meaningless. *"It is useless, useless. . . . Life is useless, all useless" (1:2).*

Allen has commented that *Crimes and Misdemeanors* contains three interlocking themes: "death," "certain moral issues" (I might rather say life's seeming amorality), and "one's position in the universe."[22] Dolores's and Levy's deaths call into question both Judah's and Cliff's attempts to carve out successful lives. Judah discovers there was "nothing behind [Dolores's] eyes," and Levy's platitudes go out the window with him. *"After all, the same fate awaits human beings and animals alike. One dies just like the other. . . . Life has no meaning for either" (3:19).* Cliff's sister is desperate for a relationship, but the man she meets through the personal ads ties her to the bed and defecates on her! Dolores opens her door expecting a deliveryman with flowers from Judah but meets her killer. Here are Allen's metaphors for life. *"I have seen everything done in this world, and I tell you, it is all useless. It is like chasing the wind. You can't straighten out what is crooked; you can't count things that aren't there" (1:14–15).*

Alone in an empty and indifferent world, might seems right! And yet *"how can anyone know what is best for us in this short, useless, life of ours—a life that passes like a shadow?" (6:12).*

Allen has repeatedly been interviewed as to his understanding of the meaning of this movie. In an interview with Stig Bjorkman, Allen comments:

> The universe is indifferent . . . so we create a fake world for ourselves, and we exist within that fake world . . . a world that, in fact, means nothing at all, when you step back. It's meaningless. But it's important that we create some sense of meaning, because no perceptible meaning exists for anybody.[23]

And so Levy seeks wisdom; Cliff, the pleasure of movies; Halley, success in her work; and Judah and Lester, riches and fame. We each create our own unique selves with our own sets of values. It's meaningless in the grand sense but important nonetheless. Allen, therefore, gives voice to an existentialist posture that seems to reside at the heart of this movie.

Originally projected with the title *Brothers, Crimes and Misdemeanors* finds its understanding of life in the existentialist vision of Dostoyevsky's *Brothers Karamazov,* a story also constructed around a murder and in which the moral structure of the universe is defined differently by three brothers. When the original title was not available for use, Allen stayed with Dostoyevsky for his signifier but took as his title a riff on the Russian's novel *Crime and Punishment.* It is again a story of a murder that gives rise both to angst and to philosophical questioning by the perpetrator.[24]

Existentialism, Ecclesiastes, and Woody Allen

Crimes and Misdemeanors' combination of angst and philosophical questioning concerning the moral order of the universe—or lack thereof—caused Rabbi Eugene Borowitz to liken Allen's prophetic skepticism not to Dostoyevsky but to a fellow Jew, Qoheleth.[25] It is not just the setting—the context of a shul, a Seder, and a Jewish wedding—that invites this comparison, however. Also central is the movie's critique of all attempts to wrest meaning from that which remains mysterious.

But as with Kurosawa, while Allen's existentialist critique has the ring of the Old Testament sage, his "solution" seems far from Qoheleth's. While Allen creates an unbridgeable chasm between God and truth, the "real" and the "reel," Ecclesiastes puts God in the center of reality. *"No matter how much you dream [Cliff], how much useless work you do [Lester], or how much you talk [Levy], you must still stand in awe of God" (5:7). "Whenever I tried to become wise and learn what goes on in the world, I realized that you could stay awake night and day and never be able to understand what God is doing. However hard you try, you will never find out. The wise may claim to know, but they don't" (8:16–17).*

While Allen suggests the importance of creating meaning because none really exists, Qoheleth counsels his readers, in the absence of any final wisdom, to enjoy the life they are given. This is because *"God has long ago approved what . . . [we] do" (9:7 NRSV). "So I realized that all we can do is be happy and do the best we can while we are still alive. All of us should eat and drink and enjoy what we have worked for. It is God's gift" (3:12–13).* God already approves of us—he created us and said it was "very good" (Gen. 1:31). Such joy is not the Pollyanna escape of Ben or the self-centered success of Lester. It is neither Cliff's retreat to the fantasy of the cinema nor Judah's "great plot." Rather, in the midst of life's chaos and amorality and fully cognizant of death as the great leveler, Qoheleth nevertheless finds in the gift of life a "useless" beauty that is to be enjoyed.

3

DEATH AND LIFE

Alan Ball and *American Beauty*

We live in a dying life.

Karl Rahner[1]

I n 2000, as the new millennium dawned, *American Beauty* was the
big winner both at the box office and at the Academy Awards.
Shot for $12.5 million, the movie grossed close to $300 million
worldwide. In Hollywood, it took best picture, best actor (Kevin
Spacey), best director (Sam Mendes), best original screenplay (Alan
Ball), and best cinematography (Conrad Hall).* Tightly written and
directed, and stunningly photographed, *American Beauty* expressed
the spirit of the times. As one critic commented, "The film is a brac-

---

*American Beauty also won three Golden Globes and six BAFTA awards (the
British equivalent to the Oscar). It was honored by the Directors Guild of America
(Sam Mendes), the Writers Guild of America (Alan Ball), the Screen Actors Guild (for
both Annette Bening and Kevin Spacey), the Grammy Awards (nominated for best
soundtrack album), and the American Society of Cinematographers (Conrad Hall),
in addition to being placed on over two hundred top 10 lists for 1999.

ing and biting comedy of American emptiness that's both sad and corrosively funny and has about it the air of a millennial classic. As it sends its characters scrambling after this or that false god . . . it gets the new season off to an invigorating start."[2] The movie is more than just a satiric critique of the American dream, however. Paradoxically, a fragile joy is also apparent. It is, in fact, this battered optimism that rang true for countless viewers who found themselves sitting in stunned silence as the film ended. Moviegoers were provided a narrative that helped them "see" life's uselessness in a new light.

American Beauty tells the story of Lester, Carolyn, and Jane Burnham, a family living the American dream—an idyllic, suburban, upper-middle-class life. But behind this rosy veneer, all is not well. As the movie opens, Lester sets the stage by means of a voice-over. He tells us as we gaze from above over his town, "This is my life." He introduces us to his family. Carolyn, his wife, "used to be happy," he says. "We used to be happy." His daughter, Jane, is, he thinks, a typical teenager, "angry, insecure, confused." "I wish I could tell her it's all going to pass, but I don't want to lie to her." He continues, "Both my wife and daughter think I'm this gigantic loser. And they are right. I have lost something. I'm not exactly sure what it is. But you know what? It's never too late to get it back." Here is the quest—the movie's theme: We are to follow Lester as he seeks to reconnect with life.

Like the artificially bred, scentless American Beauty roses that Carolyn tends in her front yard while wearing designer clogs that match her garden shears, the lives of the Burnhams are a veneer, perfect to look at on the outside but lacking any real smell or scent—any soul.* Lester is burned out in his job, trapped in a loveless marriage, and unable to communicate with his teenage daughter. *"Vanity of vanities! All is vanity" (1:2 NRSV).* Lester is one of the walking dead. He tells his boss while quitting his job, "Brad, for fourteen years I've been a whore of the advertising industry. The only way I could save myself now is if I start firebombing." And firebomb he does.

---

*The American Beauty rose is a hybrid that, in fact, lacks any real scent.

Lester Burnham (Kevin Spacey) and his wife, Carolyn (Annette Bening), argue over his new lifestyle. *American Beauty* (d. Mendes, 1999). Photo by Lorey Sebastian. © 1999 Dreamworks LLC. All rights reserved.

American Beauty tells the story of Lester's revelation of both his death in life and, ironically, his life in and through death. In his opening monologue, Lester tells us that he will be dead in a year. But he says, "Of course, I don't know that yet." We, as the viewing public, are thus informed from the beginning of the urgency of Lester's story. We also sense that we are being told Lester's story from a privileged position. Lester is looking back on his life in terms of a truth later learned. The movie is the chronicle of his rediscovery of life's meaning, even amid life's ongoing meaning-lessness. But this insight comes to him only at the end of his year of struggle.

The life that is initially portrayed in *American Beauty* is a life of green lawns, manicured roses, designer labels, fake smiles, marketing mania, and corporate greed. It looks like a bright sun-shiny world, but there is an overriding darkness to it (one that is reinforced by the movie's lighting and shadows as characters are often filmed partially in darkness). Though the song "Bali Ha'i" might be playing as musak while the family eats together, theirs is no idyllic paradise. Says Alan Ball, the movie's screenwriter, we have been led to believe that wealth and success and materialism ("stuff," as Lester will call it) will make people happy. "That is just an out-an-out lie."[3] Or as the author of Ecclesiastes informs us, *"I considered all that my hands had done and the toil I had spent in doing it, and again, all was vanity and a chasing after wind" (2:11 NRSV).*

At one level, the movie is about just that, chasing after wind. It is a frontal attack on the absurdity of American, materialistic values. It follows in the tradition of Mike Nichols's *The Graduate* (1967), Oliver Stone's *Wall Street* (1987), Ang Lee's *The Ice Storm* (1997), David Fincher's *Fight Club* (1999), and a host of other films that have critiqued the American dream. *"There may be no limit to the number of people a king rules; when he is gone, no one will be grateful for what he has done. It is useless. It is like chasing the wind" (4:16).*

Carolyn, perhaps more than any other, embodies the bankruptcy of this way of life. We watch her slap herself in the face, trying to muster a "winning attitude." We see her give herself sexually to Buddy King, the successful but crass real estate agent, because she craves what he represents—he is the "king of the hill." But success eludes her. We see her driving home from the shooting range, where she has experienced the newly found adrenaline rush of firing a pistol, singing along with the radio, "Don't rain on my parade." But rain it does (both figuratively and, in the final long sequence, literally). When Carolyn tries to help her daughter, Jane, better cope with life, she can only opine, "You're old enough now to learn the most important lesson in life. You cannot count on anyone except yourself. . . . It's sad but true, and the sooner you learn it the better." Rather than the American dream, hers has become an American nightmare. *"If someone is alone and falls, it's just too bad, because there is no one to help him" (4:10).*

Lester, on the other hand, has learned to question this American way of life. He doesn't know what is to take the place of his present lifestyle, but he is willing to seek something, anything, else. After quitting his job, he buys a bright red 1970 Pontiac Firebird, the car he has always wanted. He smokes pot, starts working out with barbells to get a sexy body that he thinks his daughter's girlfriend, Angela, will like, and takes a mindless job selling Mr. Smiley hamburgers at a fast-food restaurant. His hero becomes Ricky, the seventeen-year-old who lives next door, who casually quits his part-time catering job when his boss reprimands him for talking to Lester in the parking lot.

Lester's initial steps are, to be sure, regressive and self-indulgent. "Eat, drink, and be merry." He recalls the summer after college as the highlight of his life—he "partied and got laid. . . . It was great." But such a life is more reactive than proactive. Lester has no real clue what to do, only what not to do. When Carolyn comes home one afternoon, Lester asks his frustrated wife, "When did you become so joyless?" Of course, Carolyn's immediate response is, "There's plenty of joy in my life." But viewers know otherwise, despite Carolyn's secret affair with Buddy King. Lester's question to his wife is not meant harshly. In fact, Lester reaches out to touch Carolyn, one wounded person seeking another. He is hoping to rekindle some of the passion they once had for each other. Carolyn quenches the fire even before it ignites, however, saying as Lester tries to kiss her, "Lester, you're gonna spill beer on the [expensive] couch." Lester can only respond, "This isn't life. It's just stuff. And it's become more important to you than living. Well, honey, that's just nuts."

Despite the movie's dark humor and biting satire, despite its frontal assault on America's materialism and individualism, the film offers a sympathetic portrayal of the Burnhams.* We ache for Lester and Carolyn. They have needed something, anything, to believe in—whether money or status or sexuality. They have worked at making life produce for them. But life has proven futile. And so, *"[Lester] hated all [his] toil in which [he] had toiled*

---

*Conrad Hall, the cinematographer, recalls his first meeting with the director, Sam Mendes: "When I interviewed for the film, I told Sam that I loved the script, but I was very concerned with how we were going to ultimately like these characters. They were all so quirky, dysfunctional and basically *unlikable* people. However, Sam said if we didn't like these characters, we were in deep, dark trouble and couldn't possibly have a successful film. He made it clear to me that it was quite simple to like these characters by examining my own psyche—he asked if there weren't deep dark areas within myself that I perhaps didn't necessarily act out on, but felt nonetheless. It then became quite easy to identify [with] a lot of their dysfunctionality, because it's within us, too" (quoted in David Heuring, Jay Holben, Christopher Probst, and Patricia Thomson, "Impeccable Images," *American Cinematographer* 81, no. 6 [June 2000]: 75).

under the sun" (2:18). Like the American Beauty rose, their lives have no smell, no scent, no soul, and it is no small accomplishment for Lester to recognize this. In fact, it is only at the movie's ninety-minute mark that Lester can finally understand the saying "Today is the first day of the rest of your life." The music playing in the background as Lester leaves the house to jog, to get into better shape, is the Who's "The Seeker." Lester is still trying to figure out his life. Quitting his job is not enough, but it is a start. He has become a seeker.

Though Lester has yet to make the discovery, viewers have already been given a hint as to where meaning will be discovered, for alongside the story of Lester and Carolyn, we have been shown the parallel story of Jane, the Burnham's daughter, and her relationships with Angela and Ricky. Ricky, the neighbor boy, has an abusive father who is an ex-marine sergeant and a near comatose mother who has been psychologically beaten into submission by her husband. In seeking to control his son, the father has previously committed Ricky to a psychiatric ward, even though Ricky is sane. He repeatedly tries to force obedience by beating his son and subjects Ricky to random urine tests to check him for drugs. Unable to live life freely, Ricky retreats to taking videos of it. The first time we see him, in fact, he is videotaping Jane. Jane, for her part, has also retreated from life, unable to face her loveless, driven parents or compete with her good-looking cheerleader friend. These two outsiders, Ricky and Jane, discover each other. *"Two are better than one" (4:9)*.

Seeking a deeper connection with each other, Ricky shows Jane the most beautiful thing he has ever videotaped—a clip of a chilly, fall day when the air was electric. As Ricky and Jane watch the tape, a plastic bag remains suspended in the air, dancing in the wind. Ricky says to Jane as they watch the floating bag, "This bag was just . . . dancing with me . . . like a little kid begging me to play with it. . . . That's the day I realized there was this entire life behind things and this incredibly benevolent force that wanted me to know there was no reason to be afraid . . . ever." Ricky admits that "video is a poor excuse . . . but it helps me remember. I need to remember. . . . Sometimes, there's so much beauty in the world I feel like I can't take it . . . and my heart, she's going to cave in."*

In this way, viewers are being prepared for a choice, even before Lester himself is let in on the options. There are two forms of beauty in life, two attempts at shalom (wholeness, peace, well-being)—the American Beauty rose (whether the carefully cultivated ones in Carolyn's garden or the petals enveloping Angela's naked body in Lester's "angelic" vision) and the plastic bag floating in the wind.

On the surface, this does not seem like a real choice. The latter is so ephemeral and lacks any significance in and of itself. The bag seems useless, so dependent on the *ruach* (a Hebrew word Qoheleth uses over and over that means "wind" or "spirit"). Why chase it? The other can be produced by using "eggshells and Miracle-Gro," as Carolyn tells her neighbor Jim. Or perhaps by working out with barbells. One is ephemeral; the other is tangible and potentially perfect, something one can work to produce and take pride in. But appearances are deceiving, as Jane and Ricky know too well from their own life experiences. One needs to "look closer," as the movie trailer invites.

When given the choice between these alternate beauties, Jane knows what is real—where truth, beauty, and goodness reside—and her transformation begins. Soon after viewing the plastic bag on tape, Jane is at her bedroom window, looking across the yard at Ricky while he again tapes her from his window. On the soundtrack we hear the same haunting music that was playing while the plastic bag was floating in the air. Jane proceeds to take off her blouse and bra so Ricky can see her body. This is not a lurid act; she is not Angela, and Ricky is not Lester lusting after her. Rather, expressing both trust and vulnerability, Jane invites Ricky to look closer—to see the same fragile beauty as with the plastic bag.† And Ricky responds ap-

---

*It is worth noting that Alan Ball inserted the scene of the plastic bag floating in the air into the screenplay based on an experience he actually had. Ball says of that moment, some may think "it's just the wind." But for Ball, as for Ricky, it was more. Ball says, "I suddenly felt this completely unexpected sense of peace and wonder" (quoted in Bob Longino, "'Beauty' Maker," *Atlanta Journal-Constitution*, March 26, 2000, sec. L, p. 4).

†Earlier in the film we see Jane going online to check out breast enhancement surgery. She is embarrassed by the uneven look of her breasts. But now in their imperfection, a beauty is revealed that is life transforming.

propriately, reframing the video to focus only on Jane's face—a sign of his care for her as a person and not simply as an object of desire. Jane's mother, Carolyn, had counseled her moments before not to trust anyone, but Jane knows better: *"If it is cold, two can sleep together and stay warm, but how can you keep warm by yourself?" (4:11).*

If Carolyn shows the bankruptcy of the American dream within her generation, it is the cheerleader, Angela, who embodies the futility of that dream among teenagers. Carolyn's temptation is materialism (to do something—to grow American Beauty roses); Angela's temptation is popularity (to be someone—to be an American beauty). She desperately wants to avoid being ordinary, but as a result, she has become all tease and no substance. For a time Jane is taken in, and so too her father. (Part of Lester's wake-up call is, in fact, the lust he discovers he has for her while watching her perform a cheerleading routine at a basketball game.) But Jane learns better. Angela can't understand what Jane sees in Ricky. "He's a freak," she tells Jane. Jane yells back, "Well, so am I." Jane knows that she, like Ricky, can never be part of the American dream, but now she doesn't want to be. With a newfound self-confidence that Ricky has helped her discover, she chides Angela, "You're just too perfect." But like Carolyn, Angela doesn't yet understand how useless her beauty is, or that it is okay to be less than perfect. "Wow . . . well, at least I'm not ugly," she retorts, only for Ricky to blurt out the hurtful truth: "Yes, you are, and you're boring and you're ordinary and you know it." *"This is all that I have learned: God made us plain and simple, but we have made ourselves very complicated" (7:29).*

Crushed by the harsh truth, Angela retreats to the adulation of Jane's father, Lester. Just when the mutual seduction is to happen, however, Angela confesses that she is all bluster and bluff, that she is in fact still a virgin. Awakening from the temptation, Lester refuses Angela's sexual offer (or is it statutory rape?), providing fatherly consolation and friendship instead.

At first not understanding this fragile gift of friendship, this ephemeral expression of the wind-blown plastic bag, Angela cries to Lester, "I thought you said I was beautiful. . . . I feel so stupid." But Lester's hard-won acceptance of responsibility for his actions and his genuine fatherly care for Angela prove a breakthrough for both of them. Here, in Angela's vulnerability and authenticity, is that "alternate beauty" he now seeks to nurture. Lester asks Angela how Jane is doing, and Angela responds, "She's happy. . . . She thinks she's in love." Angela then asks Lester, "How are you?" a question no one has bothered to ask him for a very long time. And Lester responds, "I'm great! Great!" In offering the gift of life to another, Lester finds himself awakened to his own.

After Angela excuses herself for a moment, Lester sits alone at his kitchen table, looking at a photograph of his family. It is the same photograph he had looked at with pain and failure as the movie opened. But now there is a smile of joy on his face—"Man, oh, man," he quietly exclaims. No, he doesn't need to find meaning in the beauty of a blond nymph with a rose petal covering. There is more than enough joy in the ordinary. His life flashes before his eyes. He has memories of lying on his back watching falling leaves and shooting stars, of his grandmother's papery hands and a brand-new Firebird, of his young daughter at Halloween, and of Carolyn laughing at a carnival. Life is a gift to be cherished. *"So I am convinced that we should enjoy ourselves, because the only pleasure we have in this life is eating and drinking and enjoying ourselves. We can at least do this as we labor during the life that God has given us in this world" (8:15).*

Lester's insight comes on a dark, rainy night, just as he is shot in cold blood in the head. *"I realized another thing, that in this world fast runners do not always win the races, and the brave do not always win the battles. The wise do not always earn a living, intelligent people do not always get rich, and capable people do not always rise to high positions. Bad luck happens to everyone" (9:11).* But the look of contentment on Lester's face cannot be removed, even by the bullet that splatters his "rose" red blood against the white kitchen wall. As the movie ends, we hear Lester in another voice-over, one that complements and transforms the one heard in the opening scene: "It's hard to stay mad when there's so much beauty in the world." Lester says that, given life, his "heart fills up like a balloon that's about to burst . . . and then I remember to relax and stop trying to hold on to it, and then it flows through me like rain. And I can't feel anything but gratitude for every single moment of my stupid little life."

The storms of life have been seen for what they also are, a life-giving rain that invigorates and refreshes: *"Go ahead—eat your food and be happy; drink your wine and be cheerful. It's all right with God. Always look happy and cheerful. Enjoy life with the one you love, as long as you live the useless life that God has given you in this world. Enjoy every useless day of it, because that is all you will get for all your trouble" (9:7–9).*

Finding Beauty:
A Rereading of Ecclesiastes

Can *American Beauty* help us read Ecclesiastes with fresh eyes? Hopefully, this brief narration has been enough to suggest that they may walk on the same "holy" ground, or at least take parallel paths. Structurally, both begin with a poetic reflection on life's vanity and end with a complementing reflection on life's precious but fleeting beauty. In this way, both ask their audience to "see" beneath the mundane rather than foolishly try to remake it. *American Beauty* asks its viewers to "look closer." Qoheleth uses the Hebrew verb *ra'ah,* "to see," forty-seven times in his brief book. Thematically, their advice is similar too. Both do not want us to see life either as a project we can manage or as it merely appears on the surface. Rather, *American Beauty* and Ecclesiastes have a deeper intention. They invite us to see life paradoxically, not only in its bleakness but also in its transcendent beauty.

In filming *American Beauty,* Conrad Hall, the cinematographer, who had previously won an Oscar for *Butch Cassidy and the Sundance Kid* (1969) as well as seven other Oscar nominations, helped viewers to see these different takes on the world by using three distinct cinematic styles. To show the folly of our misguided attempts at making life work to our advantage, he created through his photography a series of "jail cells" in which Lester and his family lived. Shot after shot is framed to suggest that the characters are prisoners in their own home. They are unable to escape their meaningless existences. Whether viewed in the shower, in his cubicle at work, through the drive-in window, at the dining room table, or through the divided window frame of his garage, Lester is portrayed as being trapped. We see Jane similarly framed by the "bars" of her window. And we watch Carolyn sing "Don't rain on my parade" while "enclosed" in her Mercedes SUV. Lighting and set design also contribute to this sense of constriction. The surroundings are typically sparse, and the characters are often filmed in partial shadow or darkness. We as viewers are invited to observe the sterility and bleakness of life "under the sun." All our toil is vain: *"I have also learned why people work so hard to succeed: it is because they envy the things their neighbors have. But it is useless. It is like chasing the wind" (4:4).*

When Lester enters the fantasy world of his lust, the bars of the window through which he has watched Carolyn manicuring her red roses give way to erotic images of rose petals cascading out from Angela's blouse or filling a steamy bathtub in which his "angel" is bathing. The confines are gone, the photography is lush, and the colors are vivid. We are, in this way, invited to engage viscerally in his dreams, being both attracted to and repelled by what the screen is suggesting. Despite her beauty, how could a father think of seducing his daughter's friend? How alluring and yet fatal are such visions of self-aggrandizement. *"It is better to be satisfied with what you have than to be always wanting something else" (6:9).*

Finally, *American Beauty* contains pictures within the picture, shots that are filmed by the characters themselves using Ricky's handheld camcorder. These compositions are often similar to those of the painter René Magritte: images seen in the reflection of mirrors, on the TV monitor, or in the viewfinder itself. We are being invited both literally and metaphorically to see reality in a new way. Although the pictures have a grainy realism and often a dark and/or seemingly irrelevant subject matter (a homeless woman frozen to death, a dead bird, a plastic bag, a super close-up of Jane), they also have a surreal, surprising beauty that invites empathetic attention. As Ricky explained to Jane about the wind-blown bag, there is an entire life beneath and behind things, an "incredibly benevolent force" that wants him never to be afraid, ever. The haunting almost mystical music that plays during these sections reinforces what we see. *"The best thing we can do is eat and drink and enjoy what we have earned. And yet, I realized that even this comes from God" (2:24).*

In *American Beauty,* the photography itself, therefore, invites us to see life's options and to choose between differing images of reality. What kind of beauty do we see? And how do we apprehend it? Do we look with melancholy from a distance through the window to see the American Beauties that Carolyn prunes and that constantly fill the vases in the Burnhams' house? But how is it that such perfection is so sterile? Do we regressively and self-indulgently imagine the world in our own image, created for our own purposes, as Lester does while draping his "angel" with rose petals or Carolyn does while having an affair with Buddy King? Such seductions prove vacuous if not destructive. Neither attempt, whether to control or to escape life, provides the sense of shalom (wholeness, peace, and contentment) that Lester truly desires.

American Beauty, instead, provides a third viewpoint, one seen through the eyes of a handheld camcorder as it gazes at the commonplace things of life, chief of which is death itself. Having been taught by its video images to "look closer," to see beneath the surface, Ricky and Jane are able to see beyond (or inside?) life's horror. As Ricky explains to Jane about the video of the homeless woman frozen to death, "When you see something like that, it's just like God is looking right at you, just for a second. And if you're careful, you can look right back." Here is the clue to understanding the final scene in the movie as well. Gazing at the same red color as the American Beauty roses, but this time in the pool of blood from Lester's fatal gunshot, Ricky and Jane discover a transcendent stare on Lester's contented face. They do not see merely "death in life"; they also observe "life in death." Lester has found pleasure in the fact that Jane is in love. He has helped Angela better accept herself. And he has been able to respond honestly to Angela's question about how he is by saying, "I'm great! Great!" Lester's search has come to a successful end, however paradoxical and mysterious the final "shot" might seem. After all, "we live in a dying life."[4] *"It is better to go to a home where there is mourning than to one where there is a party, because the living should always remind themselves that death is waiting for us all" (7:2).*

Death, a Window into Life

When asked why he writes, Alan Ball, the screenwriter, responded, "Because it teaches me what I really believe."[5] Part of that lesson had to do with his coming to terms with death. When Ball was thirteen, he was in the car his sister was driving when she was killed in a car accident. She was driving him to a piano lesson, and it was her twenty-second birthday. Six years later, his father died at home of lung cancer. Ball, therefore, continues to "write from the heart."[6] His question is the most basic of existential queries: How are we to understand life's vagaries and absurdities, chief of which is death itself? His answer: Life is a gift of priceless yet mysterious beauty.

The importance of death as a window into life continued as a theme for Ball beyond his screenplay for *American Beauty.* It is central as well to his award-winning television show on HBO, *Six Feet Under.* The program revolves around the dysfunctional Fisher family, who runs a funeral home. Every episode begins with a corpse, hardly a promising way to start. But as Marc Peyser, the critic for *Newsweek,* recognizes, "This satirical, sometimes disturbing TV show manages to turn loose into laughter and lessons of love."[7] In one episode, Harold Mossback has a fatal heart attack on a bus while on a trip through Seattle. When David Fisher tells Mossback's daughter, who has come to make the funeral arrangements, that he can have her father's body flown back to Los Angeles, she is shocked: "Dad won't fly." David then suggests that he can be shipped via rail or freight, only for her brother to ask David, "Like FedEx?"

We laugh at the ludicrous dialogue but also in the face of death. And in the laughter, we are reminded that the gift of life is precious, however fleeting. As viewers, we struggle with the Fishers as they seek to make sense of their world. Much of what goes on is dark, even bitter, but the humanity that is revealed through humor and pain is contagious. As Rachel Griffiths, who plays the girlfriend of one of the brothers, says, "Somehow Alan is able to put the darkest, bitterest, most complex things into a meal that people are not afraid of eating. There's a whole level of spiritual inquiry that no other TV show has."[8] To see the beauty of that grace that sustains us is often too much for us. We hide in the mundane or in our fantasy worlds. It's easier to go about our daily lives, filling the hours with empty tasks or idle dreams, than to realize we are on the way toward death.

When interviewed about the show, Ball recalls the death of his sister, Mary Ann. "I still look at my life as before and after. All of a sudden I lost the person I was closest to. That's the dilemma for these characters, too. They are so deeply aware of loss, but at the same time, they have to take the risk. You have to love with all your heart, knowing that it's transitory."[9]

The longing for love, which is at the heart of *Six Feet Under,* is just as central in *American Beauty.* Through most of the movie, Lester's is a narcissistic world. It is only when he realizes that a sexual encounter with Angela will hurt her—when, that is, he chooses to care about someone more than himself—that he discovers enjoyment and contentment within himself. This, in turn, leads to a recovery of love for his daughter, Jane, and his wife, Carolyn. The final credits reinforce this message. As the names of those who worked on the movie scroll by, we hear Eliot Smith sing a Beatles' song:

The Fisher family (Lauren Ambrose, Peter Krause, Frances Conroy, and Michael C. Hall). *Six Feet Under* (writer Ball, 2000–present). Photo by Larry Watson. © HBO. All rights reserved.

Because the world is round
Because the wind is high it blows my mind
Because the wind is high
Love is old, love is new
Love is all, love is you

Because the sky is blue it makes me cry
Because the sky is blue

Here is a fragile beauty, a battered joy, that can withstand even the winds of life.

Central to the narrative of life is a fundamental paradox, one that links life and death, joy and sadness, despair and hope, earth and sky, the mundane and the transcendent. There is in life a sacred presence, which shines in and through even the bleakest human experience. Life has a sacramental quality, despite (or because of) its commonness, or so Lester Burnham and his teenage avatar, Ricky, suggest. To see life well *(ra'ah btov)* is to see behind and through it to Reality. Here, surely, is a parallel to the wisdom Ecclesiastes offers. Looking back at the end of his life with a full realization of death as the great leveler, Qoheleth must criticize the vanity, the uselessness, of all attempts to wrest meaning from life by our own efforts—whether by wisdom, wealth, or work. But though Qoheleth can be biting in his sarcasm, though his tone is often so dark that readers mistake it for pessimism or cynicism, this Old Testament sage can in the same breath advise his students:

> Go ahead—eat your food and be happy; drink your wine and be cheerful. It's all right with God [a better translation is, "for God already approves what you do," referring to the Book of Genesis, where God made us and called the result "very good"]. Always look happy and cheerful. Enjoy life with the one you love, as long as you live the useless life that God has given you in this world. Enjoy every useless day of it, because that is all you will get for all your trouble. Work hard at whatever you do, because there will be no action, no thought, no knowledge, no wisdom in the world of the dead—and that is where you are going.
>
> 9:7–10

Qoheleth recognizes that much frustrates life—life's amorality, life's opaqueness, and most of all death itself. Given such reality, it would have been better, from one perspective, if we had never been born. But by viewing this same reality from a different vantage point, we see that life also is precious. It has so much useless beauty. As Qoheleth recognizes, *"A live dog is better off than a dead lion" (9:4)*. We must speak of *both* life's futility and its wonder. In fact, we must speak of them in the same breath.

It is significant that the transcendent vision of life in both Ecclesiastes and *American Beauty* comes without reference to the church or the synagogue, without reference to traditional religion. This is perhaps why the medieval church saw Ecclesiastes as a dangerous book. Although Qoheleth, writing late in Israel's history, knew the law (the story of God's gracious provision for his people at the Red Sea and at Mt. Sinai), he chose not to use it in his argument until the final coda. As a Jew, Qoheleth had this "answer" to life's vanity in his theological quiver. He could have talked about the God of the exodus who rescued and redeemed his people and gave them the law. He could have spoken of how Yahweh time after time rescued his people from catastrophe. But he didn't. A revelatory trump card is not played. Readers can only conjecture as to why. Perhaps Qoheleth did not want to reinforce the religious smugness of his people, something that lay behind their falsely understood "gospel of prosperity." Just as money, celebrity, wisdom, and pleasure can be a means of shutting out God's transforming presence, so too can creeds and dogmas. Believers can be smug!

Qoheleth, therefore, did not appeal to the law in his main remarks. To correct the arrogance of his readers, he instead turned to the ultimate leveler, death. Here, paradoxically, is a perspective for life. Qoheleth's recognition of life's ultimate uselessness allowed him to see life's grandeur and beauty. It is only life's seeming meaninglessness that reveals life's meaningfulness. Such is the paradox of life. Here, we might say, is the real American Beauty—a useless beauty on which all our hopes must be placed. It is more ephemeral than even the rose, but it is also real. Here is a beauty providing hope and perspective for all else.

4

THE SADDEST HAPPY ENDING

Paul Thomas Anderson
and *Magnolia*

I put my heart—every embarrassing thing that I wanted to say—in
"Magnolia."

Paul Thomas Anderson[1]

A s the millennium turned, a new group of young, creative
filmmakers emerged: Wes Anderson *(The Royal Tenenbaums)*,
Kevin Smith *(Dogma)*, Spike Jonze *(Being John Malkovich)*,
Andy and Larry Wachowski *(The Matrix)*, Alexander Payne *(Election)*, Tom Tykwer *(Run Lola Run)*, Darren Aronofsky *(Pi)*, and
Paul Thomas Anderson *(Magnolia)*, among others. These writer-
directors *(auteurs)*, like other contemporary pop culture artists, are
fascinated with mixing genres and often use a nonlinear, rapid-fire
style of storytelling. They draw inspiration from old TV shows and
music videos, ads, music, the Internet, and even video games. They

are largely self-taught, having chosen not to attend film school but rather to eat, drink, and sleep movies.

Paul Thomas Anderson went to see *E.T.* as a kid and started dressing like Henry Thomas. After he saw *Rocky,* he began running every morning and drinking five raw eggs at breakfast. Whenever he eats mashed potatoes, he says he still thinks of *Close Encounters.* Says Anderson, "I never had a backup plan other than directing films."[2] Anderson's father was a TV host in Cleveland for late-night horror movies before moving to Los Angeles and becoming a voice-over actor. He gave Paul his first video camera before he reached his teens, and Anderson shot a thirty-minute video, *The Dirk Diggler Story* (1988), before he graduated from high school. This would become the prototype for *Boogie Nights.*

Viewers find in Anderson's movies a set of paradoxes. He is, for example, a visual stylist, but much of his inspiration comes from music, which also plays a central role in his films. Anderson has chosen to use his own backyard in a suburb of Los Angeles—the San Fernando Valley—as the setting for most of his movies. Yet he refuses to make his neighborhood into another "character." His movies have more of a universal than a local quality to them; they are about people everywhere. Anderson uses raw language and R-rated themes. His movie *Boogie Nights* is centered in the porn industry, while the showpiece of *Magnolia* is a macho seminar on how to pick up women through intimidation. Yet a moral imperative runs throughout his films. An incisive critic of late-twentieth-century America, he is also a romantic, in his words, "a sucker for the human element."[3]

Magnolia

> I was trying to say something with this film without actually screaming the message.
>
> Paul Thomas Anderson[4]

On the surface, *Magnolia* is a melodrama about larger-than-life characters whose parallel lives intersect through coincidence, death, ambition, and dreams. It is filled with frailty, betrayal, and turmoil. Yet the movie is paradoxically lyrical and hopeful. Viewers sense a profound wisdom, even if events don't always make sense. The movie not only is honest about the human condition, with its mystery, amorality, and death, but also recognizes the need to try to set things right. As John C. Reilly, who plays the well-meaning but bungling cop Jim Kurring, comments about the script, "I had a really emotional response to it. I think Paul has a remarkable ability for capturing the little human details of life and at the same time presenting a very big perspective on humanity at large. It's the perfect kind of millennial movie, I think, an intense investigation into what really drives us and the distance between who we think we are and who we really are."[5]

Magnolia is set on Magnolia Boulevard in the San Fernando Valley and takes place during one twenty-four hour period in 1999. In rapid-fire, frenetic succession, the movie dips into the lives of nine individuals in the opening montage. Overlaid is the music, "One is the loneliest number that you'll ever do,"* which unifies the scene. All the characters are searching for meaning in life, or at least some happiness, given their lack of loving relationships. One is listening to his ad in a personals dating service; another is giving an infomercial about how to dominate a woman sexually; a third is snorting coke and having sex with a casual pickup from a bar; still another is listening to his dad harass him; another is almost beside herself as she watches her husband die. All would like to start life again, but it isn't that easy. As the narrator later puts it, "The Book says, 'we may be through with the past,' but the past ain't through with us."

At the center of the seemingly diverse but interconnected group is an elderly TV producer, Earl Partridge (Jason Robards), who is dying of cancer. There is a deeper cancer, however: Earlier in his life

---

*Anderson's films are primarily character driven. He says, "I begin writing with a list of the characters' traits, everything about them. Most studios begin with a concept and then fill in the characters, which are often generic. The great films give you a person, or people, and their world. That's my goal" (Paul Thomas Anderson, quoted in Lynn Hirschberg, "His Way," *New York Times Magazine* (December 1999): 1, www.ptanderson.com/articlesandinterviews/nytimesmagazine.html.

he abandoned his wife and let his fourteen-year-old son care for her alone as she, too, died of cancer. His trophy wife, Linda (Julianne Moore), married him for his money but now realizes as he is dying that she has come to love him. The money isn't worth it anymore. She wants to give Earl drugs to end his pain as a way of atoning for her promiscuity and deceit. Phil Parma (Philip Seymour Hoffman), Earl's nurse, is trying to help his patient reconnect with his estranged son, Frank T. J. Mackey (Tom Cruise), a disgustingly chauvinistic, self-help guru whose motivational seminar is called "Seduce and Destroy." (His phone number is 1-877-TAMEHER.)*

A second constellation of characters revolves around Jimmy Gator (Philip Baker Hall). He has broadcast over twelve thousand hours on television and has been host of one of Earl Partridge's programs, *What Do Kids Know?* for over thirty years. Jimmy is estranged from his daughter, Claudia Wilson (Melora Walters), a drug addict totally devoid of self-worth, who is struggling in the aftermath of sexual abuse by her father.† Jim Kurring (John C. Reilly) meets her while answering a routine domestic disturbance call—her music is too loud. A Christian who prays, he knows his job is tough, but he is happy if he can even occasionally help someone. Meanwhile, we see Stanley Spector (Jeremy Blackman), the current whiz kid, browbeaten by his father, who is hoping for riches. We are also introduced to Donnie Smith (William H. Macy), a former winner on the show who is now a mediocre appliance salesman, lonely and bitter toward his parents, who stole his quiz show earnings.

Such a listing is hard to keep straight. Much of the movie is a melange of intersecting stories that connect only through chance and coincidence and whose full nature is not evident until much of

---

*At the time of the movie's initial release, viewers who called this number listened to a message from Frank.

†Anderson says with regards to Jimmy Gator, "It's the first time when I've been able, at the end of a film, to hate one of my characters. There truly is a sense of moral judgment at work with this character. I can't even let him kill himself at the end—he's got to burn. . . . With this character, I'm saying 'No.' No to any kind of forgiveness for him" (Paul Thomas Anderson, *Magnolia: The Shooting Script* [New York: Newmarket Press, 2000], 201).

the way through the movie. But as the movie cuts in and out of the lives of these nine individuals and other supporting cast members, viewers discover relationships between the vignettes that point to a greater interconnectedness in all our lives.

Most of the characters also have a dramatic opposite. Thus, much of what happens is "repeated" in another guise. Both Earl Partridge and Jimmy Gator are dying of cancer and have estranged children who wish them to be dead. We fear that Stanley, the young whiz kid, will follow in the pathetic steps of Donnie Smith. The nurse, Phil Parma, and the policeman, Jim Kurring, are very different kinds of caregivers, but both, while bumbling, are instruments of love and grace in the movie. *"What has happened before will happen again. What has been done before will be done again. There is nothing new in the whole world" (1:9)*

Moviegoers are prepared for this mysterious interweaving of lives by the audacious and lengthy prelude Anderson attaches to his movie. He opens the film with "footage from old newsreels," purporting to show three examples of mind-boggling coincidences, all of which involve death. These stories, based on urban legends, are told by an uncredited Ricky Jay (a magician who in real life hosts a TV show about strange but true occurrences) with a detail and a precision that make them believable. One has to do with three men—Green, Berry, and Hill—who murder a man on Greenberry Hill. A second recounts the story of a blackjack dealer from Reno, Delmar Darion, who is scuba diving in Lake Tahoe and is unceremoniously removed from the lake by the water scoop of a firefighting plane and deposited dead in a tree. The pilot had ironically had a fight with Delmar in a casino the day before and feels so guilty about this random killing that he in turn commits suicide.

The third vignette has to do with a son who tries to commit suicide by leaping off a roof, only to be killed by a shotgun blast as he falls past the window of his apartment before landing in a construction net that would have saved his life. The gun was accidentally fired by his mother, who was once again threatening her husband with what she thought was an unloaded gun. The son had purportedly loaded the gun, hoping one of his parents would shoot the other and end the ongoing, unpleasant arguments. The narrator concludes his reflections on all three events by saying, "And it is the humble opinion of this narrator that this is not just something that happened. This cannot be 'one of those things.' This, please, cannot be that. . . . This was not just a matter of chance. . . . These strange things happen all the time."

Vanity of Vanities

"Again I saw that under the sun the race is not to the swift, nor the battle to the strong, nor bread to the wise, nor riches to the intelligent, nor favor to the skillful; but time and chance happen to them all" (9:11 NRSV).

"Time and chance" happen to us all. But in *Magnolia*, Anderson weaves a tapestry that suggests that meaning can emerge from what otherwise would seem to be coincidence and loss. As the lives of his characters are presented much like a collage, it is clear that neither power nor money nor fame nor wisdom bring meaning and satisfaction to life. Earl Partridge might have once been a powerful, rich TV executive, but now he is a shell of a man who is dying of cancer, alone with his regrets. *"We leave this world just as we entered it—with nothing. In spite of all our work there is nothing we can take with us" (5:15).* Jimmy Gator is still a famous TV icon, a model of wholesomeness and wisdom to his public, but his ego, his infidelities, and his sordid family relationships now betray another darker story. *"Someone may rise from poverty to become king of his country, or go from prison to the throne, but if in his old age he is too foolish to take advice, he is not as well off as a young man who is poor but intelligent" (4:13–14).*

Frank T. J. Mackey tells his seminar participants that relationships with women are all about power—"seduce and destroy." He says to his students, "I will not apologize for who I am. I will not apologize for what I need. I will not apologize for what I want." *"I had all the women a man could want. . . . Anything I wanted, I got. I did not deny myself any pleasure. I was proud of everything I had worked for, and all this was my reward" (2:8, 10).* Frank teaches that to manipulate women, you must fake being a nice and caring person. But he has no answer for the woman TV reporter (April

Grace—note the name!) who discovers that he has lied both about attending the University of California and about his mother still being alive. *"If you dig a pit, you fall in it; if you break through a wall, a snake bites you" (10:8).* Tellingly, April Grace breaks through Frank's façade, pointing him toward the truth.

Linda, Earl's gold-digging wife, has everything—diamonds, a fur coat, the inheritance. But when she realizes Earl is dying, none of that seems important. Instead, her duplicity eats at her soul. *"I discovered that laughter is foolish, that pleasure does you no good" (2:2).* Stanley's father is also consumed by only one thing, the money his son can win. So he's willing to do what seems necessary to make his son perform. He berates his son, hits him, bribes him. Life is lost in the process. As Stanley tells him at the movie's end, "Dad, you have to be nicer to me." But it seems too late, at least for his father. *"If you love money, you will never be satisfied; if you long to be rich, you will never get all you want. It is useless" (5:10).* Donnie Smith was a household name after winning the quiz show as a kid, but his adult life is a mess. He lacks the ability even to hold his job as a salesman for Solomon Electronics. He can only dream of having enough money for orthodontics so that he will be attractive enough to be of interest to a good-looking bartender. *" 'So what have I gained from being so wise?' 'Nothing,' I answered, 'not a thing' " (2:15).*

A Different Wisdom

Anticipating America's fascination with *Who Wants to Be a Millionaire?* (or mirroring the long-running *Jeopardy*), the plot weaves in and out of the television game show *What Do Kids Know?* (the longest-running quiz show in America that pits brainy kids against adults). Stanley Spector is the current child prodigy, but as already noted, all is not well for him. At home he must endure a father who constantly berates him and seems little interested in anything but his son's cash prizes. One of the former quiz kids, Donnie Smith, lacks friends and direction. The show's host (Jimmy Gator) and its producer (Earl Partridge) are both dying of cancer and do not have a clue about life. *"We labor, trying to catch the wind, and what do we get? We have to live our lives in darkness and grief, worried, angry, and sick" (5:16–17).*

Frank T. J. Mackey, the son of the dying television patriarch, has rebelled against his father's desertion by deserting him. When the nurse (Phil Parma) who is trying to help Frank's dying father locate his son calls Frank's assistant, he suggests, "You know the scene in which the dying man tries to get in touch with his long-lost son. . . . This is the scene." Like many of us, Phil understands his existence in terms of "life the movie."[6] Anderson himself reflects:

> I'm a product of growing up on movies, but when the movies betray you and haven't taught you how to feel something or what to do—for instance, if someone in your life dies—it's flabbergasting because the movies haven't shown you how to deal with that. . . . Movies are a big influence on how we deal with death, with family relationships, and I wanted to show that. But they can also be a complete betrayal in terms of how to live your life.[7]

"It is better to have wise people reprimand you than to have stupid people sing your praises" (7:5). There is a need for a wisdom that goes beyond what TV and the movies provide.

The need for a wisdom that goes beyond cultural values is at the heart of *Magnolia.* The movie is humorously divided into sections by several weather forecasts—our wisdom is as reliable as the weatherman's, it seems. Television and movies are portrayed as providing both the content and the paradigms for much of our everyday knowledge of life. But these are sometimes inadequate. As the narrator concludes at the movie's end, returning to his description of the three unlikely happenings, "There are stories of coincidence and chance and intersections and strange things told. . . . And we generally say, 'Well, if that was in a movie I wouldn't believe it.' . . . And it is in the humble opinion of this narrator that strange things happen all the time."

In *Magnolia,* Anderson has appropriated music as well as TV and movies to portray the possibilities and limits of wisdom. In fact, a song by the singer-songwriter Aimee Mann, "Wise Up," was his initial inspiration for the script. Anderson says, "I really set out to write an adaptation of her songs. . . . She's like the way Simon and Garfunkel were to *The Graduate* or Cat Stevens to *Harold and Maude*. Her songs become the built-in voice of the movie, tying all the stories together."[8]

In an audacious move that serves as the emotional heart of the movie, Anderson weaves together the lives of his chief characters by having them serially sing lines of the same song. They sing in their individual settings of their need to "Wise Up," and yet the effect is that of a corporate voice. This happens two and a half hours into the movie, after the tragedies of the characters' lives have become all too apparent. With the characters at the end of their ropes and rain falling outside and Earl having been humanely given a lethal dose of morphine by Phil to ease his death, we hear Claudia, the game show host's daughter, softly begin to sing "Wise Up." Then we cut to Jim Kurring, the bumbling, lonely cop, who picks up the lyrics. And on it goes. First Jimmy Gator, then Donnie, then Phil and Earl, then Frank, then Stanley singing in succession:

> It's not what you thought
> when you first began it.
> You've got what you want,
> Now you can hardly stand it,
> But now you know it's not going to stop
> 'til you wise up.
> It's not going to stop
> 'til you wise up.
> Prepare a list of what you need,
> before you sign away the deed.
> It's not going to stop,
> so just give up.

The song connects the characters with one another and with the audience in ways that story structure and dialogue cannot. It reveals that they are at the same point in their transformation process. Anderson comments on the song: "Hopefully it unifies everything, calms everything down and feels completely natural. Haven't you ever sung along to a song on the radio? In the simplest way, it's just that. . . . I thought it was going to be something very sweet, sentimental in the best way. I didn't consider it outlandish. And I still don't."[9]

Magnolia invites us all to wise up by looking deeper—by finding a wisdom that defies our traditional human agendas, whether power, fame, pleasure, or knowledge. But this proves difficult. Even after we hear the cast of characters singing of the need to wise up, each still tries to save himself or herself by his or her own effort. Jimmy destroys what little is left of his relationship with his wife, Rose, with his brutal, self-serving honesty. (He will do anything to escape his guilt.) Donnie tries to steal money for braces. Claudia sniffs coke to gain the courage to see Jim. Frank lashes out angrily at Earl. But though these characters continue to try to manage their fate, their actions are but last gasps. They sense (and we the audience know) the futility of such attempts to produce meaning. *"It is useless, useless" (1:2).*

No human agendas suffice. Our rationalistic assumptions prove hollow. Nowhere is this clearer than in the movie's climax, when a prolonged shower of frogs stops people in their tracks. The rain of frogs, however absurd, actually becomes a catalyst for good. The falling frogs awaken Earl from his coma/stupor long enough for him to acknowledge the presence of his son, Frank. Jim, the cop, assists Donnie after he is knocked off a building by the pelting frogs and then helps him return the money he has stolen. The frogs bring Claudia and her mother together once again. The frogs defy logic to be sure, but then so does life. As Stanley comments, reflecting the prologue's earlier observation, "It happens. This is something that happens."* Set up for this miraculous shower of frogs by the amazing coincidences that led off the movie, characters and viewers alike are forced to confront a reality beyond their ability to control.

Magnolia has literally given us a riff on "it's raining cats and dogs." Anderson says he got the idea for the frogs from reading the books of Charles Fort. (Those watching carefully will note that Stanley

---

*The same conclusion is offered by the painting on the wall of Claudia's apartment. Its caption, which alludes indirectly to her own abuse by her father, reads, "But it did happen."

is reading one of Fort's books in the library as he prepares for the quiz show.) Fort lived from 1874 to 1932 and spent his adult life collecting accounts of mysterious incidents that he hoped would undermine humanity's confidence in science as the end all and be all. Sea monsters, ghosts, mysterious lights, live creatures falling from the sky—all these were a fascination to Fort. But showers of frogs were his favorite. Fort (and Anderson) sensed that modernity feigned control and understanding only by ignoring what it couldn't figure out.

After the shower of frogs was put into the movie, Anderson was told about its similarity to one of the plagues in the Bible, and so Anderson added this referent to his movie as well. Three signs in the movie contain the reference Exodus 8:2. The text reads, "If you refuse [to let them go], I will punish your country by covering it with frogs." Biblically, the plague of frogs functions as a divine offering of liberation from oppression for those who have eyes to see and ears to hear. And the frogs function similarly for Earl and Frank, for Donnie and Claudia. A supernatural intervention, they are an offer to wise up, to realize that we cannot save ourselves. *"No matter how much you dream, how much useless work you do, or how much you talk, you must still stand in awe of God" (5:7).*

Given the vanities of life—chief of which is death itself—given circumstances that defy human planning and control, the movie invites us to recognize the importance of love and forgiveness. Money, fame, pleasure, surface knowledge, and power will prove hollow. Given *"time and chance" (9:11),* even the best efforts prove futile. We should, instead, *"enjoy life with the one you love, as long as you live the useless life that God has given you in this world" (9:9).* What remains in *Magnolia,* when all else is recognized as *"chasing the wind" (2:17),* are relationships. Frank needs to regain his true masculinity by reconnecting with his father, something Phil Parma gracefully assists. Stanley needs to find the courage to confront his dad, hoping against hope that a new relationship is possible. Linda, who has recognized her love for Earl too late to experience his forgiveness, will have the opportunity to connect with Earl's son, Frank, who visits her in the hospital. Donnie, who has sought to fulfill his sexual fantasies but has yet to find a relationship he can

Jim Kurring (John C. Reilly) and Claudia Wilson Gator (Melora Walters) in *Magnolia* (d. P. T. Anderson, 1999). Photo by Peter Sorel. © 1999 New Line Cinema. All rights reserved.

give himself to, can nevertheless confess to Jim Kurring, "I thought he'd love me if I got braces. I really do have love to give. I just don't know where to put it." Reality has taken the place of fantasy. It is, for Donnie, a start. *"Two are better off than one, because together they can work more effectively. If one of them falls down, the other can help him up" (4:9–10).*

Jim Kurring, who assists Donnie, has himself struggled with how to love. When we first meet him, he is using the personal ads to seek someone "who likes quiet things." But ironically, when he meets Claudia, even though it is because of a domestic disturbance call, he senses that she is someone who needs love and whom he can love. Claudia is so insecure that she asks him after their first date, "Now that I've met you, would you object to never seeing me again?" But with an affection for her that defies logic, Jim remains committed. As the movie ends, Aimee Mann's song "Save Me" is heard in the background: "You look like the perfect fit, / a girl in need of a tourniquet." And Jim offers just that. "Can you save me / come on and save me," the song pleads. As the song continues, "If you could save me / from the ranks of the freaks / who suspect they could never love anyone," Jim is with Claudia in her bedroom. We hear his voice on top of the song, "You are a good and beautiful person." The camera focuses on Claudia and stays there as she struggles to accept his gift of love. Miraculously, she smiles briefly for the first time, and the movie ends.* *"Only the wise know what things really mean. Wisdom makes them smile and makes their frowns disappear" (8:1).*

Rather than being merely a series of vignettes, *Magnolia's* nine stories ultimately play out with one voice. Unified by the music that initially inspired it, the story moves painfully from "One is the loneliest number that you'll ever do" to a recognition of the need to "Wise Up" to a fragile acceptance of the gift of another's care—"Save Me." The movie thus presents through music and image a coherent understanding of life, one rooted in others and quickened by the reality of death. It is a wisdom at odds with much of our modern agenda. Dark yet hopeful, *Magnolia* helps viewers confront their pasts and risk living in an uncertain future. It provides "the saddest happy ending."

Anderson's Other Movies

Paul Thomas Anderson was only twenty-four when he was invited to develop a feature film as part of Sundance's Filmmakers Workshop. The result, *Sydney* (1996; *Hard Eight* for its USA release), starring Gwyneth Paltrow and Samuel L. Jackson, tells the story of four persons involved in the Reno gambling scene. Unfortunately, the studio with which Anderson was working tried to recut the movie, and he felt his work was being ruined. The fact that Anderson was allowed to submit his original print of the movie to the Cannes Film Festival, where it was accepted, forced

---

*When asked if there is some sort of hope for the two of them at the end of *Magnolia* or if "all the sadness" is not going to stop, Anderson replied, "For me the writer, Yes, it equals totally cathartic, and totally hopeful, and Yes! They are going to get together at the end! . . . But in no way is it going to be easy or entirely possible. But it is a surrender to falling in love, no matter how much s— that's going to entail. . . . I do lean toward the side of happiness, but . . . it's not that simple" (Anderson, *Magnolia*, 207).

the studio to let Anderson finish the movie as he desired. But with little if any money assigned for its promotion, the movie was seen by few and had little effect.

It was not Anderson's initial movie, therefore, but his second that established him as a major new talent. *Boogie Nights* came out in 1997, and it contained a number of themes and techniques that would be repeated in other guises in *Magnolia*. He chose, for example, edgy subject matter. *Boogie Nights* is set in the late 1970s and early 1980s when the glory days of pornography as "art film" *(Deep Throat, The Devil in Miss Jones)* gave way almost overnight to quickly shot videos for home and hotel room that focused on little more than the sex act itself. Though of necessity R-rated, given its context and crude language, the movie is not exhibitionist or even particularly sexy. The story is more about the people than the profession.

The movie's opening scene moves from a neon sign of a disco to a pulsing nightclub where in three minutes we observe eight of the main characters. In the mass of revelers, it is not clear who are extras and who will prove central to the story. As in *Magnolia*, the background music, "Best of My Love," unifies what otherwise seems random. We meet, among others, porn producer Jack Horner (Burt Reynolds) and his live-in porn queen, Amber Waves (Julianne Moore); the teenage waitress Rollergirl (Heather Graham), whom Jack recruits; and the well-endowed teenage busboy Eddie Adams (Mark Wahlberg), who longs for fame and fortune to escape his abusive home.

Boogie Nights is in an odd sort of way a rags-to-riches story, telling how Eddie chases his dreams through X-rated movies and finds a new "family" among porn veterans. Renaming himself Dirk Diggler after seeing the name in big lights in a dream, he lives the life of a star, counting on his "one special thing" (an oversized penis) to see him through. As the disco rhythms and campy 1970s fashions suggest, life is meant to be fun. And for a time it is. Dirk is a stud in all ways. Fame and money come easily and with them possessions and power. But these also prove corrupting. The endless celebration comes to an end at a 1979 New Year's Eve party. The decade is over, both literally and figuratively. At the party, Amber introduces young Dirk to drugs, Jack is warned of the changes video will bring, and an assistant shoots his promiscuous wife and her latest lover before turning the gun on himself. In the second half of the film, we watch as "the wages of sin" play out for most of the characters, most notably Dirk. He becomes the prodigal son, but unlike in the biblical story, when Dirk rejoins his "family" in the porn business, there is no real forgiveness or redemption. Life continues, but only after a fashion.

The movie is in some ways a morality tale. Decadence will slide into decline. One "family" member kills his wife; another is arrested for child porn. Drugs contribute to Dirk's downfall, making him unable to do his job. Self-deception is rampant. And even the movie's coda does not erase the suspicion that all is not well with Dirk. When queried as to whether the ending was meant to be redemptive, Anderson responded, "But after this whole journey, what have they learned? If that's happy and redemptive, OK."[10] The hedonism, greed, and violence that are portrayed have no future. Dirk's "reel" family is not "real," despite the reunion. *"Vanity of vanities! All is vanity" (1:2 NRSV).*

It is not just Dirk who has dreams that prove a "chasing after wind." Jack Horner had wanted more than anything to elevate porn film to art. ("It is my dream to make a film that is true and right and dramatic," he says.) After viewing a scene from his latest, artless Dirk Diggler film, he rhapsodizes, "This is the best work we've ever done. . . . This is the film I want them to remember me by." But in the end, the video industry has reduced his work to just one coupling after another. Story and acting do not matter. Given her work, Amber Waves has been judged an unfit mother and has lost custody of her son. So she dreams of being a "mother to those who need love," those like Eddie and Rollergirl. There is a poignancy in her desperate, den-mother existence. But it is Eddie's dreams, in particular, that we follow. He had posters of supermodels and Corvettes in his bedroom at home, and we watch him live in and out of these fantasies. His ambition, he says at the height of his hubris, is to be the sole "King of Dirk." *"Anything I wanted, I got. I did not deny myself any pleasure. I was proud of everything I had worked for, and all this was my reward. Then . . . I realized that it didn't mean a thing. It was like chasing the wind—of no use at all. After all, a king can only do what previous kings have done" (2:10–12).*

As in *Magnolia,* Anderson is brilliant in using the outlandish to illuminate the everyday. The characters that make up his exaggerated world might be on the edge of society, but their concerns are also ours—reputation, the good life, happiness. And the consequences that befall them are applicable to us as well. To help us make this connection, particularly given his voyeuristic (and at times salacious) story, Anderson uses popular music from the 1970s. His musical score pulls viewers in, commenting on and extending the movie's meaning. Just as in *Magnolia,* in which Anderson uses the songs "One," "Wise Up," and "Save Me" to interpret the images and dialogue that fill the screen, Anderson uses music to dialogue with the images in *Boogie Nights.* The top 40 songs throughout the movie function as they might in a musical, providing commentary on what is going on.[11] We hear, for example, the song "Lonely Boy" as we watch Amber miss a phone call from her son because he asked for her by her unknown but actual name, Maggie. Or again, as the movie unravels near the end, we hear the lyrics, "Sail away on the crest of a wave. . . . It's magic." But there is little "magic" left to be seen on the screen.

Boogie Nights exposes the vanity of life for many living in the 1970s. The golden age of irresponsibility proved to be anything but golden. Fame, looks, money, pleasure—such dreams are pathetically deluded. Anderson does not need to include either the controlling presence of organized crime in the porn industry or the impending AIDS epidemic to make his point. Moviegoers leave the theater with a sense of pathos for the characters but with little hope. The "saddest happy ending" does not quite arrive.

Both *Boogie Nights* and *Magnolia* are lengthy dramas with ensemble casts whose confused characters try to cope with arbitrary circumstances and wrong choices, with mixed results. They are Anderson's "novels." With *Punch Drunk Love* (2002), viewers have a chance to view an Anderson "short story," in which the focus is narrower. In particular, Anderson says that after living through the making of *Magnolia,* he realized, "I would really like to take a left turn and make myself happy, get rid of all this cancer and crying."[12] Only ninety-seven minutes in length, *Punch Drunk Love* is billed as a romantic comedy, but it is like no other romantic comedy ever made. It is a genre bender, something on the edge. As with *Magnolia,* it is a movie whose lightness is seen over against an ever-present darkness.

Anderson has given us a stylized fable in which love is pitted against life's absurdity and pain. And love triumphs brilliantly. Anderson's same concerns are present—absurdity, pain, love—but they have been modulated from a minor to a major key. The plot is typical Anderson, replete with lonely characters, bizarre events, and surprising caregivers. As in his other movies, the setting is the San Fernando Valley with its strip malls and industrial parks. Adam Sandler is Barry Egan, a socially maladjusted salesman of novelty toilet plungers who is obsessed with buying three thousand dollars' worth of Healthy Choice Pudding so he can collect over a million frequent flier miles (even though he has yet to fly). Sandler plays the same moronic presence he has become famous for (in movies such as *Happy Gilmore, Big Daddy,* and *Waterboy*), an innocent man who is prone to violent moods. But this time, Anderson invites viewers to look closer, to see the loneliness and anger lurking behind Sandler's exterior.

Barry is overwhelmed by life until three random circumstances conspire to offer him a new life: An SUV careens down an abandoned street before flipping over, but Barry hardly notices. A shuttle van mysteriously stops, lowers its steps, and deposits a harmonium, which Barry quickly brings inside and tries to fix. And Lena (Emily Watson), a coworker of one of Barry's seven abusive sisters, shows up at the warehouse and falls in love with him (for no apparent reason).

As in Anderson's other movies, Barry's ongoing concern is with how to connect in a disconnected world. Seeking any kind of relationship to overcome his deep loneliness, Barry unwisely calls a phone-sex line in a moment of despair. The girl on the line, after taking his credit card number, tells Barry, "You don't have to be lonely now. You have me." But Barry knows, as we do, that there is no solution to life's absurdity here. The call leads to comic relief, as four brothers from Utah reappear throughout the movie, hired by the phone hotline owner to try to blackmail Barry for money. But the call also leads eventually to a deeper insight for Barry.

Faced with the real possibility of harm or even death, Barry makes a split-second decision both to value what he has and also to defend it. In an eventual showdown with the crooked but self-righteous phone-sex entrepreneur (Philip Seymour Hoffman), Barry declares, "I have a love in my life that makes me stronger than anything you can imagine." Coming from the shy, social misfit Barry Egan, the comment gets a laugh, but its idealism is offered without apology. As Roger Ebert said with regard to *Magnolia,* Anderson's "extroverted self-confidence . . . rejects the timid postmodernism of the 1990s." His movies do not "apologize for their exuberance, or shield themselves with irony against suspicions of sincerity."[13]

Again, as in *Magnolia,* music is important, providing clues to the meaning of *Punch Drunk Love.* Jon Brion's score is romantic one moment, percussive the next. Just like life! Even in the dialogue, music provides clues, at times, as to how we are to understand the story. Barry's bright-blue suit, for example, elicits the question from everyone he meets, "What's up with the suit?" Barry has no answer, but for Anderson and other movie aficionados, it is a reference to MGM musicals such as *Singin' in the Rain* in which somebody is always wearing a bright blue suit.[14] *Punch Drunk Love* is just such

Barry Egan (Adam Sandler) and Lena (Emily Watson) fall in love. *Punch Drunk Love* (d. P. T. Anderson, 2002).

a musical, in an odd sort of way. Barry and Lena do indeed learn to sing in the rain. Anderson also uses the harmonium as a metaphor for Barry's life. Though it mysteriously arrives on Barry's doorstep, it must be repaired before it can be played. This is, analogously, what Lena's pure love also accomplishes in Barry. Though the dark might remain, love, like music, is playing in and through him. Having been trusted and thus able to trust another, Barry can move gingerly beyond his isolation and destructive anger to embrace life. A loser has become a winner.

Embracing Life

Philip Seymour Hoffman has acted in each of Anderson's four movies. On the *Magnolia* DVD, he comments on the wisdom embedded in that film: "The whole movie's riddled with this feeling that anything could happen at any moment. You could die or you could discover something that changes everything. So whatever you think it is you need to be doing in life, you better start doing it."[15] Here is Anderson's take on life.

This wisdom is similar to that found in Ecclesiastes. *"Time and chance" (9:11)* happen to us all. Life is often unfair (*"You find wickedness where justice and right ought to be" [3:16]*); it is certainly a mystery (*"How can anyone know what is best for us in this short, useless life of ours?" [6:12]*); and death is a reality we all face (*"The same fate is waiting for us all" [2:14]*). Given that this is our *"lot" (3:19 NRSV)*, all our efforts to produce a meaningful life will fail. Money, fame, wisdom, sex, power are all *"chasing the wind" (2:26)*. Yet consistent with the writer of Ecclesiastes, Anderson can also affirm that *"it is good to be able to enjoy the pleasant light of day. Be grateful for every year you live. No matter how long you live, remember that you will be dead much longer. There is nothing at all to look forward to" (11:7–8)*. This "saddest happy ending" is enabled not by self-striving but by the gracefulness of another who cares (*"If it is cold, two can sleep together and stay warm" [4:11]*).

5

CHANCE AND FATE

Tom Tykwer and *Run Lola Run*

Again I saw that under the sun the race is not to the swift . . . nor
favor to the skillful; but time and chance happen to them all.

Ecclesiastes 9:11 NRSV

L ike Paul Thomas Anderson, Tom Tykwer (pronounced Tick-
ver) has lived and breathed movies since he was a little kid.
He reflects, "Mine is one of those ridiculous careers where I
didn't seem to have a choice. The only things that I learned were
about films. I'm a specialized person, and luckily, fate welcomed
me."[1] Tykwer's enthusiasm for film was so passionate that by age
eleven he had shot a short film, by thirteen he was working in a
cinema, and at twenty-three he ran an art house cinema in Berlin.
He says that he still "goes to see films, if it's possible, every day."[2]
Also like Anderson, Tykwer had no formal training as a filmmaker,
having been rejected for film school. Instead, he learned his craft
by imbibing movies themselves.

Tykwer's films are filled with allusions to movies by such filmmakers as Alfred Hitchcock and Krzysztof Kieslowski. But they also are filled with experimental visuals and bold musical accompaniment that owe more to MTV than to the classics—the mix of 35 mm with video, jump cuts, rapid-fire montages, whip pans, fast and slow motion, crane shots, cartoons, bold color and color filters, split screen, and the like.

Tykwer is sometimes called the German *Wunderkind* who helped usher in the third wave of German cinema. Each new creative period for German filmmakers has followed major transformations in society. Fritz Lang and F. W. Murnau sought through their expressionistic Weimar Cinema to give people a new identity following World War I. Rainer Werner Fassbinder, Wim Wenders, and Werner Herzog were among the postwar generation who in the 1960s and 1970s attempted to reinvent cinema in Germany after a lapse of twenty-five years. Now a decade after the reunification of East and West, Tykwer is helping to invigorate young filmmakers in Germany through both his own movies and the artist-driven production company X-Filme, in which three of the four partners are directors.[3]

Tykwer has directed five feature films, four of which have been released in the United States. *Run Lola Run* (1999) put him on the map. Made for under $2 million, it earned over $7 million in art house receipts and quickly achieved cult status among postmoderns. (Its DVD remains extremely popular.) This led quickly to the 2000 American release of an earlier movie, *Winter Sleepers* (1997), followed by *The Princess and the Warrior* in 2001 and *Heaven* in 2002. Tykwer not only directs but also writes his own screenplays and even collaborates in the music's creation. The only script he did not write is *Heaven*, written instead by the late Polish master Krzysztof Kieslowski, who gave us the *Decalogue* and the Three Colours trilogy *(Red, White,* and *Blue)*. Even in this case, however, Tykwer says that "by the time I had finished reading the third page, I had forgotten about who had written it. I became immersed in the screenplay as if it were my own. I knew exactly what the story was getting at—not just explicitly, but implicitly as well, atmospherically, beyond the moral conflicts and the narrative circumstances. . . . I was able to see myself reflected in it."[4]

All of Tykwer's movies, including *Heaven,* have, in fact, a common sensibility rooted in a common vision of life. Tykwer says he is interested in "love, fate, freewill."[5] Perhaps one could say that Tykwer is interested in exploring both chance and choice in relationship to fate, particularly as it plays out in love. His typical movie includes wounded and lonely outcasts who are brought together by circumstances and passion that together suggest larger patterns of fate. Although one of the two lead characters may initially be stronger, both partners are running toward a new life. After a variety of false solutions are tried, the movies end hopefully, with love conquering crime, death revealing life, and the future wonderfully open as the couple walk/drive/fly into the sunset. Fate never becomes a fatalism for Tykwer.

In bringing to life this common plotline, Tykwer combines a neo-romantic sense of life and a hyper-real observation of it. He considers movies to "have two sides, the analytical and the poetical," and he observes, "I love movies that deliver both."[6] So too do Tykwer's audiences, who are often transfixed by his juxtaposition of the earthy and the ethereal, the kinetic and the slow, the pounding beat and the eerie silence. Though his characters might seem, given life's troubling circumstances, to be merely chasing the wind (Hebrew, *ruach*), they instead discover the Spirit (in Hebrew, also *ruach*) filling them.

Run Lola Run

Most of us spend our time crawling, groping, climbing, sometimes running, but always moving like the works of a clock. But now and then joy comes to arrest the motion, it stops the tedious ticking of our life-clocks with the bracing discovery that we have received a gift. It works most magnificently when we feel our own life as if it were God's gift to us.

Lewis Smedes, *How Can It Be All Right When Everything Is All Wrong?*

In *Run Lola Run,* Tykwer takes one of the oldest of questions regarding the meaning of human life (What is our fate given time and chance?) and makes it the theme of a postmodern movie. Tykwer says in his DVD commentary that the subject he was interested in exploring in this movie was how fate and coincidence intertwine with each other and "how a very, very small situation can change your whole life forever and push it into a completely different direction."[7] His plot is simple, while the variations and experimentation in storytelling create interest and suggest meaning. The story starts with a phone call from a desperate Manni (Moritz Bleibtreu) to his girlfriend Lola (Franka Potente). "Help me, Lola. . . . I don't know what to do." Manni, a courier for a smuggler, has managed to leave a bag containing 100,000 deutsche marks (about $60,000) on the subway, and a bum has absconded with it. Expected to deliver the money to his boss in just twenty minutes, Manni is frantic. He fears that if he turns up empty-handed, he will be killed. What follows is Lola's (and Manni's) passionate attempt to get the money and beat the clock.

When things don't work out the first time, the viewer is surprised to discover that, as with a video game, the scenario is merely reset and the "game" is replayed. In this way, the movie provides three runthroughs in its short ninety minutes. *What has happened before will happen again. What has been done before will be done again. There is nothing new in the whole world" (1:9)*. Given that there is only twenty minutes to finish the "game"—to hatch a plan, navigate various physical obstacles, deal with circumstances and people, and get the money to Manni—everything moves at breakneck speed, providing little time for character development. The repeated telling of a simple story has been done before: Peter Howitt's *Sliding Doors* and Krzysztof Kieslowski's *Blind Chance* come to mind. The effect is to show how random circumstances encourage new choices that transform the same plot, altering the fate of the characters in the process.

In between the three tellings of the twenty-minute sprint are two lyrical interludes that reveal something of the emotional depth between Manni and Lola. The driving beat of the repeated sequences together with these slower meditations on love and death parallel the musical pattern of a rave party, in which the frenzy of 140 beats per minute is juxtaposed with lyrical songs that provide relief and perspective. These romantic pauses are filmed with a red light (the color of both love and death) and probe the questions, Do you love me? (Lola) and Will you remember me when I die? (Manni). Manni and Lola are typical young adults struggling to find their place "under the sun," and their questions are those that countless others have asked. We identify with them.

Tykwer's mix of media does not stop with his use of these filtered interludes. Switching back and forth between video and 35 mm film, live action and animation, color and black-and-white, his stunning visuals combine with breathtaking music to create an atmosphere that captivates the viewer. So too does Tykwer's fascination with how even the smallest of circumstances changes all that follows. The audience soon begins to look for both what has changed and what the characters remember from one segment to the next. Reinforcing this discovery process is a series of rapid-fire flash cuts that scroll in a few seconds through the future of characters Lola encounters along the way. These "Polaroids" reveal how the lives of these characters might be different because of a change in circumstances.

In the first two tellings of the story, Manni and Lola both try to manipulate circumstances to produce a favorable destiny. But caught in the vortex of city life in Berlin, they face obstacles and institutions that intervene to frustrate their endeavors. Parents, financial institutions, and religious figures are all indifferent or powerless. At the beginning of the movie, the characters are introduced using mugshots, suggesting something of the prison they find themselves in, and this proves to be both Lola's and Manni's experience. In the first sequence, when Lola does not arrive in time with the money, Manni chooses to rob a store. The tragic result is that Lola is fatally shot.

In the second sequence, Lola is so frustrated by both her father's infidelity and his indifference to her that she pulls the gun from the security guard's holster and robs the bank. Circumstances again work against her, however, for though she arrives in time, Manni is hit by an ambulance and killed before Lola can give him the money. It does not seem to be the case that what Lola wants, Lola will get. *"Like birds suddenly caught in a trap, like fish caught in a net, we are trapped at some evil moment when we least expect it" (9:12).*

The setup for *Run Lola Run* has suggested what the movie will be about: *"Time and chance happen to [us] all" (9:11 NRSV).** As

---

*Ironically, this reflection in Ecclesiastes on the universality of time and chance has as its reference 9:11 (9/11).

the movie opens, the pendulum of a giant clock swings back and forth, and we hear the incessant tick of a clock. The camera travels up the clock to its face, where the hands are moving rapidly. We then enter the world of the film through the gaping mouth of a monster above the clock dial and watch in animation as Lola runs into a vortex with sharks' teeth and centipedes intruding. We are, all of us, being swallowed up by time.

The opening of the movie also raises questions regarding life's randomness. We see people, most of whom are out of focus, milling around aimlessly in a field. All we can know, says a man who comes into focus (the bank security guard whom we later meet), is "the ball is round. The game lasts ninety minutes. That's a fact. Everything else is pure theory." But then as he kicks the ball high into the air, as if to start the game, the thousands of people randomly milling around are seen from above, their bodies spelling out the title of the movie in German, *Lola Rennt.* There is a mysterious larger pattern in life, despite the seeming chaos.

This theme—that the workings of time and chance reveal fate—(not fatalism) becomes clear in Lola's third attempt to "play the game." Lola meets the same characters as she speeds along, but she is unable to get the money. Having come to the end of her rope, she is forced to look beyond what she herself can produce. With ethereal music playing in the background, we hear Lola's inner voice as she closes her eyes while still running: "Come on. Come on. . . . Help me. Help me. . . . I'll just keep on running, okay? . . . I'm waiting. . . . I'm waiting." This inchoate "prayer" is not tied to any religious tradition or institution, but it is clearly spiritual in its intention. Rather than look at life as simply a task (German, *Aufgabe*) to be accomplished, Lola recognizes that her task is dependent on life's gift (German, *Gabe*).

Caught up in her thoughts, Lola is almost run over by a large truck. Startled into a recognition of her surroundings by the angry cries of the truck driver—"Wake up! You almost were killed!"—she notices a casino across the street. Shot in a way reminiscent of the faithful entering a cathedral—there is a majestic building, organ music, a dress code, attendants who keep order, parishioners who watch, even a defined "liturgy" by the croupier—Lola enters these "sacred" halls and receives the "gift of life" in the form of sufficient roulette winnings to rescue Manni. But even before this "miracle," grace is present in the hall: Having only ninety-nine deutsche marks, she is given by the woman in the money cage a 100-mark chip; being told she is not dressed properly to enter, she is nevertheless admitted; and beckoned to leave by an attendant after winning the first time, she is nonetheless allowed to wager one more time (and win again). Having given up on any attempt to create solutions where no solutions exist, she is startled to receive the needed cash as a gift. *"No matter how much you dream, how much useless work you do, or how much you talk, you must still stand in awe of God" (5:7).*

Manni, at the same time, is also receiving an unexpected gift. He gives back the phone card he has borrowed from a blind woman standing outside the booth, only for her to reach out, causing him to wait long enough to see the homeless man who has his money pass by on a bicycle.* The blind woman even seems to "look" in the direction of the man, suggesting an intentionality that is more than randomness. In this way, Manni is able to run after him and miraculously recover his lost marks, forcing the man at gunpoint to hand them over. Even more surprising, having received this unexpected gift apart from his effort (though, like Lola, he did have to run after it), Manni offers his own gift in return. He gives his gun to the man, who has wondered out loud what will be left for him if his money is taken.

For Manni, grace has begotten grace. And so, too, for Lola. Having received the unexpected earnings from the roulette wheel apart from her effort to produce a solution, Lola is running to get the money to Manni when she comes upon an ambulance at an intersection. She climbs into the back of it to hitch a ride and once again meets the bank guard, who has had a heart attack. As the attendant pumps on his chest to sustain his life, the dying man reaches out his hand. To the shock of the attendant, Lola responds and takes it, and almost immediately the rhythm of the guard's heart becomes regular. Lola's words

---

*The blind woman is played by Monica Bleibtreu, Manni's (Moritz Bleibtreu's) real-life mother.

Lola (Franka Potente) runs between a group of nuns on her way to her father's bank. *Run Lola Run* (d. Tykwer, 1998). Photo by Bernd Spauke. © 1998 Sony Pictures Enter-tainment. All rights reserved.

to the attendant, though mistranslated in the English subtitles as "I will stay with him," are "I belong to him" *("Ich gehoere zu ihm").*

The secret connection between the guard and Lola is in this way revealed. In the first run-through, we have learned that her supposed father is not in fact her father as he yells at Lola in the presence of the guard, "I'd have never fathered a weirdo like you." In the second run-through, the security guard grabs his heart after Lola takes his gun. He seems to be having heart problems. And earlier in this third rendition, after Lola yells, "Daddy, Daddy" as her father drives away, the bank guard opens the door and says, "You've come at last, dear." Lola pauses to look at the guard as if she knows him and then leaves. (Could it be that her rejection contributes to his subsequent heart attack?) Now viewers understand this enigmatic dialogue. The security guard is her real father. Having been forced to watch her grow up from a distance, he is now given back his life by her acceptance.

The movie is not yet over in terms of its surprises. Both Manni and Lola now have money sufficient to handle the crisis. When Lola arrives at their meeting place, Manni is nowhere to be seen. After standing in the middle of the street looking in all directions for him,

Lola sees Manni get out of the gangster's car, shake hands with him, and walk toward her. As the credits get ready to roll, the two of them walk off holding hands, Manni asking Lola what is in the bag. Lola has gotten the money, but it has proven to be useless. Lola will not save Manni's life; life is a pure gift. *"So I am convinced that we should enjoy ourselves, because the only pleasure we have in this life is eating and drinking and enjoying ourselves. We can at least do this as we labor during the life that God has given us in this world" (8:15).*

It might be true that everything in life is just theory, except that the ball is round and the game is ninety minutes. But it seems that choice and chance have conspired, allowing Lola to recognize that fate is grounded in a love that is life giving. With a better sense of their past and present, Manni and Lola can walk into their future as new people.

The Princess and the Warrior

> Everything that happens in this world happens at the time God chooses. . . . So I realized that all we can do is be happy and do the best we can while we are still alive.
>
> Ecclesiastes 3:1, 12

The Princess and the Warrior takes up the same theme as *Run Lola Run:* Love can reveal how chance and choice actually intertwine to become one's destiny. As in *Run Lola Run,* vehicles hit pedestrians, and there is an ambulance scene, a bank robbery, and, yes, some running. Death is again the backdrop for life, and amid the outrageous, there are moments of real tenderness.* The movie is both a

---

* *The Princess and the Warrior* is also distinct from *Run Lola Run,* particularly in its tone and pace. In *The Princess and the Warrior,* the action scenes are balanced by longer, more meditative sections in which we get to know the characters. This slower pace (the movie is forty minutes longer than *Run Lola Run*) caused one critic to rename the movie *Crawl Lola Crawl.* But as the lovers have yet to meet when the film opens, and the characters feel distant to the viewers given their emptiness and sadness, it takes time for circumstances to accumulate and relationships to be built. The more lyrical pace is therefore necessary and illumining.

romance and a thriller. Part fairy tale and part reality based, it tells the story of a woman ("the princess") on a mission to discover the man ("the warrior") who saved her life. In the process, she discovers that coincidence is grounded in fate, and therefore, in her words, "Nothing is meaningless."

Many of the same actors are present in both movies, most notably Franka Potente. This time, though, "Lola" is a mousy blond with a shuffling gate whose name is Sissi. Again she gets in trouble with the law while trying to help her boyfriend, Bodo, who, like Manni, is a petty criminal. The two lead characters, as in *Run Lola Run,* try to create a new life by their own efforts. But as in other Tykwer films, it is only when they run out of options—when they stop striving and instead begin to receive life as a gift—that things work out and they are able to drive off into the sunset. Sissi brings healing to Bodo, even as she is in the process being healed by him. Tykwer says about the two movies, "The core of both films is how passion relates to fate. . . . 'Lola' is looking at the structural potential of the subject [through plot]; the other one is looking more at the emotional conception of it [through character]."[8]

As with all such stories, Tykwer's framing of his reality-based fairy tale is crucial: "Once upon a time . . . they lived happily ever after." In the movie prologue, we see Sissi's friend Meike mailing a letter to her from a stunning house on a remote ocean cliff. There is no sound except for the faint tick of a clock. The mail is then brought to the city, and we watch from the perspective of the letter as it goes through the sorting machine. From the "once upon a time" of the idyllic countryside, we are in this way brought into the bustle of city life. Circumstances, together with wrong choices, will threaten to block out this Eden, but the dream is never totally lost. Sissi, a nurse in a psych ward, will look at Meike's pictures in the letter, for example, all the while holding a conch shell to her ear to hear the surf.

As the movie nears its climax, Sissi shares with the unbelieving Bodo, "Listen. You have to decide. I'm going to leave. You can come with me. I had a dream. We were brother/sister, father/mother, husband/wife . . . maybe it's wrong. But I thought it was happiness." Bodo responds, "I don't believe in happiness." By the story's

Sissi (Franka Potente) and Bodo (Benno Furmann) driving away from the psychiatric hospital. *The Princess and the Warrior* (d. Tykwer, 2000). Photo by Bernd Spauke.

end, however, Bodo is in fact driving with Sissi back to Meike's dreamlike cottage, escaping the city's demands. They will "live happily ever after." The filmmaker has given us his version of the myth of the garden and the machine. Life is not meant to be lived in the prisons/psych wards we have created for ourselves; there is another, more natural way. And we, the viewers, are being asked to make our choice.

If the prologue and postlude are dreamlike and ethereal, the remainder of the movie is anything but. It is, in fact, startling in its realism and intensity. We see Bodo, the troubled ex-soldier who has just been fired (for crying during a funeral at the mortuary where he worked) and whose wife has killed herself after a domestic squabble. He is fleeing from the gas station he has just robbed with workers in close pursuit. Sissi, who lives and works in a psych ward, is taking a blind patient on a walk into the city. Bodo's and Sissi's lives meet beneath a large truck (literally, the "machine") that pins Sissi to the pavement, the driver having been momentarily distracted by Bodo. When Bodo crawls under the truck to hide from his pursuers, he discovers Sissi choking on her own blood. She is unable to speak or breathe. Seeing her dying, Bodo decides to rescue her by performing a tracheotomy. Circumstance and choice thus come together as fate, and the eventual outcome is love. *"Everything that happens was already determined long ago, and we all know that you cannot argue with someone who is stronger than you" (6:10).*

The cumulative effect of the rescue's detail (it lasts over eight minutes) is overpowering—its initial silence, Sissi's inner thoughts, Bodo's terse comments, the blood, the music that becomes like an alternate narration, Sissi's blank stare, and Bodo's surprising tears. Viewers find the scene almost too intense to watch. When Bodo has sucked out some of the blood that is choking her, Sissi sees his tears and reflects, "But I don't think he was sad. I felt that if a person wasn't alone, they could find happiness in the outside world." Even the violence of life can be transformed by the caring presence of another. After taking her in the ambulance to the hospital (here is his means of escape from the police), Bodo disappears. This near-death experience has been for Sissi a taste of life. She has been given a second chance, and as a result, Bodo will eventually find his life renewed as well.

Here then is the setup. Bodo can say to his brother, "I was useful today. I saved someone's life." And Sissi, after a long but miraculous recovery, can confide in the blind man who was with her when the crash happened that she is afraid. This "seer" responds, "You're afraid everything will be the same as before." Will anything really change? That is the question. Can Bodo reconnect with life, and can Sissi find her real destiny? The movie's structure already suggests what the answer will be (they will live "happily ever after"), but the path is anything but easy. *"The same fate awaits human beings and animals alike. One dies just like the other. . . . So I realized then that the best thing we can do is enjoy what we have worked for. There is nothing else we can do" (3:19, 22).*

Events have conspired to bring this unlikely couple together, as has Bodo's decision to act on Sissi's behalf. Now it is Sissi's turn to make a choice: Her resolve becomes like steel. She tells Bodo, "I want to know if my life has to change and if you're the reason." Sissi's newfound strength is nowhere clearer (or more humorous) than when she blackmails a gun shop owner into giving her Bodo's address by having her blind companion fall down in the doorway, pretending that he has been hit by the owner. This middle section of the movie, much like *Run Lola Run,* reveals wrong choices being made, circumstances proving painful, and the two finally discovering that they cannot produce a new destiny by sheer effort alone.

The final scene plays out after the fugitives, Bodo and Sissi, are discovered hiding in the psych ward. Fleeing to the roof of the multistory building, they hold each other's hand, pause, and then jump off. The scene is reminiscent of the ending of *Thelma and Louise,* and viewers are horrified that after such a struggle, it all comes down to this. Is death the only means of liberation from society's oppression, as Bodo has feared amid his tears? The audience is left gasping in relief as the two land in a pond on the asylum's grounds and ultimately make their escape. The thin line between life and death could not be more finely (finally) drawn. Playing in the background as the couple jumps is music that reminds listeners of a clock. The sounds then turn to a high-pitched tone as if an alarm clock were going off. By their "baptism" in the pond's murky waters, Bodo and Sissi are awakened to a new life.* As if to symbolize this rebirth, the couple is shown under water in a dreamlike world, the water now crystal clear and bright.

The movie is not over, however. Again, circumstances conspire to become fate. There is unfinished business. The two stop at a gas station to fill up their car for the drive to Meike's house overlooking the ocean. It is, by chance, the same gas station where Bodo's wife killed herself by setting fire to the gasoline she was pumping while Bodo was in the restroom. Symbolically, Bodo has never been able "to get off that toilet," as his brother told him in his last words before dying. Now Bodo is able to face his demons. When he comes out of the same bathroom to get into the car with Sissi, the movie becomes surreal. There are now two Bodos. But as the three begin to drive off, the new Bodo makes his former self get out of the car.

---

*Concerning this scene, Tykwer commented that they just couldn't die: "If they had died, this would have been the most cynical thing—I hate cynical films generally" ("Interview with Tom Tykwer and Franka Potente," June 8, 2001, www.themoviechicks.com/jul2001/mcrtprincess.html).

Bodo is able to let go of his grief and guilt and move on. Sissi and Bodo can now drive into their future. Bodo gently takes Sissi's hand as they drive. Sissi turns to Bodo and feels his eyes; there are no more tears. Just as in *Magnolia*'s ending, when Claudia looks at Jim Kurring and smiles for the first time, Bodo now smiles; it is his first smile too. The epilogue showing the tranquility of the couple arriving at their Eden extends lyrically the music of Penguin Café Orchestra's "Nothing Really Blue" for a full two and a half minutes. *"Young people, enjoy your youth. Be happy while you are still young. Do what you want to do, and follow your heart's desire. . . . Don't let anything worry you or cause you pain. You aren't going to be young very long" (11:9–10).*

Heaven

Both *Run Lola Run* and *The Princess and the Warrior* explore the possibility of fate leading to happiness, of the gift of redemption through circumstance and choice for those who are struggling to move beyond death to life. The question remains, however, are some through chance or human choice left unredeemed? Can fate turn into fatalism? Is "heaven" beyond the possibility for any? Perhaps not all can live happily ever after? This is the question that Tykwer takes up in *Heaven.*

Again, Tykwer begins his movie audaciously, with an extended setup that is both horrendous and riveting. After a prologue in which a helicopter simulation takes us over green fields and the pilot asks the instructor how high he can fly, we are provided a case study on which to reflect: Is fate in reality fatalism? Cate Blanchett plays Philippa, an idealistic, British schoolteacher in Turin, Italy, who has seen her husband and some of her students killed by drugs. Her complaints to the police have produced no response. *"I have . . . noticed that in this world you find wickedness where justice and right ought to be" (3:16).* So having learned the identity of the businessman who is Turin's drug lord, she decides to try to avenge these deaths herself. She goes to his high-rise building and plants a bomb in his office, only for fate to conspire against her. The cleaning lady removes it with the trash before it goes off, and when it tragically does, it kills the worker and a father and his two young daughters who are riding the elevator with her. Soon she is arrested. Circumstances have, it seems, foiled justice and spread grief. *"Some good people may die while others live on, even though they are evil" (7:15).*

Overcome by guilt because her vigilante justice has backfired, Philippa has her tears wiped away by a policeman, a *carabiniere* by the name of Filippo (Giovanni Ribisi), who proceeds to fall hopelessly in love with her on the spot. Soon, he is orchestrating her escape. As chance would have it, his birthday was on the day of her first communion, and his brother was in her English class. Such interconnectedness might seem inconsequential, but in Tykwer's movies, "coincidence" is foundational to life's meaning and possibility. We are on familiar Tykwer terrain, watching as both the caregiver and the criminal need to break free and chance and choice conspire as fate to provide love a chance.

When Philippa tells her rescuer that she no longer believes "in sense, in justice, in life," Filippo responds, "I believe there will be something and that it will be beautiful." Escaping the prison of the city (the "machine"), they flee to the dreamlike town of Montepulciano, far removed in the countryside of Tuscany (the "garden"). By the movie's end, Filippo's dream has proven to be true. Life *"under the [Tuscan] sun" (2:11 NRSV)* is returned to its most basic simplicity. The two fugitives with nearly identical names have both shaved their heads and are dressed alike in jeans and white T-shirts. Shot from above, the two are eating ice cream while watching a wedding reception on the piazza complete with white umbrellas. Their final, playful run through the Italian countryside and their lovemaking silhouetted against a spectacular sunset reinforce that this is a return to Eden. The lovers have discovered their true humanity. *"Go, eat your bread with enjoyment, and drink your wine with a merry heart; for God has long ago [in the Garden of Eden] approved what you do. Let your garments always be white. . . . Enjoy life with the wife whom you love, all the days of your vain life that are given you under the sun, because that is your portion in life" (9:7–9 NRSV).*

The couple's final ascension into the heavens in a helicopter serves as the epilogue. It provides symmetry with the opening helicopter scene and suggests that none is beyond fate's gracious intention. It therefore proves a fitting ending. But seen from another perspective, the ascent seems atypically escapist. Philippa and Filippo have discovered heaven on earth, with fate the midwife. There is no need for their removal.

Fate, Chance, and Choice

Like other postmoderns, Tykwer's characters are suspicious of institutions (police, government, family, banks), value experience, recognize suffering as a part of life, and admit the centrality of ambiguity in their lives.[9] As the bank guard says, "The ball is round. The game lasts ninety minutes. That's a fact. Everything else is pure theory." Yet with a growing number of the younger generation, he would have us realize that circumstances need not have the final, fatalistic word, no matter how unjust and senseless our lives seem. Though Bodo might think that "it's all meaningless anyway," he discovers with Sissi that "nothing is meaningless." While Philippa responds to the twist of fate that kills a father and his two daughters by saying that she no longer believes "in sense, in justice, in life," Filippo can still reassure her: "I believe there will be something and that it will be beautiful." This "heaven" will take a variety of forms—a bank guard and his daughter being reconnected, the washing away of guilt before a drive through the woods to a seaside bungalow, a romp in the countryside.

We need not despair, but neither can we rely solely on personal resolve and choice, however courageous. Our personal strategies will prove a dead end; they will need to be replayed. When Lola robs the bank, the sequence ends with Manni being killed; so too when Manni robs the store, Lola dies. When Philippa takes justice into her own hands, only injustice results. When Bodo and his brother rob a bank to start a better life, the brother is killed.

Only as we realize that our lives are graciously undergirded by a larger spiritual presence, a fate, can we move forward in hope. Lola discovers this as she finds herself waiting and prays, "Help me. Help me." She discovers that help in a casino that symbolizes the secular equivalent of a church. Philippa finds spiritual contentment with Filippo under the Tuscan sun, and her later ascent in the helicopter is much like Job having his good life returned to him at the end of the story—nice, to be sure, but unnecessary for him, as he has already seen God. Sissi and Bodo look at each other and trust themselves to fate as they "jump off the roof" of their old life and begin again at the seaside.

Such a philosophy for life finds a parallel in Paul Tillich's theology. In his *Systematic Theology*, he delineates three approaches to reality: the heteronomous, the autonomous, and the theonomous.[10] In the first, outside factors control one's approach to life. The problem, of course, is that one loses his or her personal identity in the process, as Sissi comes to realize. In the second, one tries by an act of the will to rebel, to create a future independently. But as Philippa experiences, death is amoral; we are unable to control life by our own efforts. Instead, a third approach is demanded/invited. Only as we understand that we live supported by the gracious presence of something greater than ourselves will we discover that our lives have value by nature of their very existence. Only such a life-giving "theonomy" can provide the courage to be.

Given circumstances that conspire against them, Manni and Lola try to create a new life by their own choices, but death prevails. It is only as they accept life's gracious destiny as a gift from beyond them that they can move forward. Similarly, Sissi and Bodo are both reduced to a shell by the circumstances of life, chief of which is death. Longing for something more, they both try to escape by their own efforts. But they too find the courage to embrace their future only by accepting their destiny. Philippa and Filippo find that life's injustice and corruption are impossible to endure passively, but neither do they yield to isolated acts of heroism. Contentment, however fleeting, is possible only when they recognize that there is a beauty to life—a useless beauty—that transcends outer circumstances and inner resolve. The two lovers can accept their fate peacefully, and the result is heavenly.

Here is a wisdom that echoes that of Ecclesiastes. Qoheleth recognized that we cannot accept a simplistic view of life. He looked for answers and found none (cf. 7:28). The sage observations that his earlier colleagues had made within the wisdom tradition in Israel might be generally true. He even quotes a number of these approvingly. But such wisdom cannot be absolutized into a series of laws and maxims that will necessarily bring happiness. Afterall, *"No one knows what is going to happen next, and no one can tell us what will happen after we die" (10:14; cf. 6:12).*

Life does not follow a road map; it is, instead, mysterious and too often even amoral. There simply are too many exceptions: *"You cannot straighten out what is crooked; you can't count things that aren't there" (1:15).* *"Don't be surprised when you see that the government oppresses the poor and denies them justice and their rights" (5:8).* *"Even a king depends on the harvest" (5:9).* *"Some good people may die while others live on, even though they are evil" (7:15).* *"Dead flies can make a whole bottle of perfume stink, and a little stupidity can cancel out the greatest wisdom" (10:1).* For reasons such as these, *"in this world fast runners do not always win the races" (9:11).* *"Time and chance happen to [us] all" (9:11 RSV).* Only death is sure (9:2–3).

And yet Qoheleth can tell us, *"Here is what I have found out: the best thing we can do is eat and drink and enjoy what we have worked for during the short life that God has given us; this is our fate. If God gives us wealth and property and lets us enjoy them, we should be grateful and enjoy what we have worked for. It is a gift from God. Since God has allowed us to be happy, we will not worry too much about how short life is" (5:18–20).* Such a paradoxical view of life recognizes that although circumstances intervene and death is the great leveler, God nevertheless graciously provides. We should *"enjoy the pleasant light of day" (11:7)* while we are able.

Here, once again, we are presented with life's paradox. In Qoheleth's words, *"I thought long and hard about all this. . . . One fate comes to all alike, and this is as wrong as anything that happens in this world. As long as people live, their minds are full of evil and madness, and suddenly they die. But anyone who is alive in the world of the living has some hope; a live dog is better off than a dead lion" (9:1, 3–4).* Though life's contradictions merit the judgment that all is meaningless, it is also the case that life is precious, a gift to be cherished in wonder and hope. As Elizabeth Huwiler summarizes this ancient sage's advice, "All life is *hebel*, and yet joy is both possible and good. It is important not to make one of these claims the only message of the book and dismiss the other as either a distraction or a grudging qualification. Qohelet insists on both, and often in the same passage."[11]

6

AN AMBIGUOUS JOY

Marc Forster and *Monster's Ball*

From whence cometh song? From the tear, far away.

Theodore Roethke, "Song"

Monster's Ball is both disturbing and deeply moving, a film that stays with you long after the screen goes dark. On one level the movie is a contemporary American drama set in the deep South that deals with racism, capital punishment, familial abuse, and violent death. The movie transcends any temptation to be simply a politically correct melodrama, however. It centers its attention not on solving these social ills but on portraying the loneliness, loss, and need for personal transformation that result from them. Whether that transformation takes place and, if so, what exactly the nature of it is are the questions with which viewers are left. In the process, this movie transcends its time and place, speaking to all of us in the midst of our sadness and pain.

Monster's Ball tells the parallel stories of two people, a white prison guard, Hank Grotowski, and Leticia Musgrove, the black wife of a man he helps execute. Given the movie's setting in the segregated South, the stories of the two main characters take on added significance. Both feel trapped by what they have been given in life. When they meet by chance, they find themselves drawn together by the wounded vulnerability of their common humanity, just as we are drawn to them. Seeking solace in each other, they find, if not redemption, at least a place of shared understanding. Theirs becomes a fragile joy.

Playing Hank and Leticia are Billy Bob Thornton and Halle Berry. Each was able to draw on his or her own past experiences, both in film and in life, in shaping their roles. Thornton is known for the flawed and quirky characters he has played: a mentally impaired man in *Sling Blade;* a psychotic mechanic in *U Turn;* the slow-witted brother in *A Simple Plan;* an asocial barber in *The Man Who Wasn't There;* a racist bulldozer operator in *The Apostle.* Growing up in the South, Thornton says he believed most of the time that his father didn't like him. When he died, Thornton didn't cry but said he was relieved. Only later did he realize that his father might have been afraid of him. It was his father, Thornton says, whom he was playing in *Monster's Ball.*[1] Berry was also able to bring her life to her role. She grew up in an interracial home in which her father abused her mother until he abandoned them. She had to endure her share of racial taunts as a child, lost most of her hearing in her left ear when a boyfriend abused her, and confesses that she even thought of suicide after she split up with her husband, baseball player David Justice. Sadness and pain know no boundaries.

The creators of *Monster's Ball* were as unlikely a team as their two lead characters. But again, like Hank and Leticia, they shared a common knowledge of life's misery. Written by two out-of-work actors and first-time screenwriters, Will Rokos and Milo Addica, *Monster's Ball* was initially meant simply as a vehicle to give them some work. Having both been raised in violent homes, they decided to write about what was familiar to them. Chosen to direct the film was a thirty-one-year-old Swiss, Marc Forster. His few other films included two documentaries on child burn victims and teen suicide, as well as the limited release movie *Everything Put Together,* which had its world premiere at the 2000 Sundance Film Festival and tells the dark story of a suburban mother's isolation from friends and community after the loss of her baby from sudden infant death syndrome. Concerning his choice to do *Monster's Ball,* Forster says:

> I responded for both personal and social reasons. The issues it addresses—breaking the cycle of violence, racism and abuse—weren't presented in a preachy way, and I feel what the film is ultimately about is forgiveness and redemption. . . . I'd had a turning point in my own life. . . . There was a three-month period when my father, my brother [to suicide] and my grandmother all died. So I understood how something like that changes you in the way you see life and the way you do things.[2]

Two Monstrous Lives

As the opening credits roll for *Monster's Ball,* we see the shadow of a ceiling fan move slowly across Hank as he lies asleep in bed. One senses an uneasiness and listlessness in the air. Climbing out of bed, Hank goes to the bathroom, where he throws up. He is wearing a sleeveless undershirt, what sometimes is called a "wife beater." Without so much as a word of dialogue, viewers are let into Hank's world. The scene soon cuts to Hank's grown son, Sonny (Heath Ledger), who is having impersonal sex with a prostitute in a motel room.* There is no eye contact and little dialogue. Sadness, distance, and loneliness are all that is evident. Soon we meet Hank's father, Buck (Peter Boyle). With his nose plugged into an oxygen tank, he is cutting out an article to add to his scrapbook on executions: "Lawrence Musgrove Dies Tonight." Over breakfast Buck demands that Hank run two black children off their property who are just then walking up the drive. Calling them "niggers,"

---

*The scene was shot in the actual motel room where Jimmy Swaggart was caught having sex.

he complains that they no longer know their place. Though Hank seems mildly uncomfortable with such obscenities, he nonetheless obeys his father, taking his shotgun outside to scare off the boys. Viewers are thus ushered into the world of the Grotowskis, three generations of prison guards who live together yet alone. *"I have seen everything done in this world, and I tell you, it is all useless. It is like chasing the wind. You can't straighten out what is crooked; you can't count things that aren't there" (1:14–15).*

Life seems largely devoid of meaning for Hank. His one joy, or at least his coping mechanism, is eating chocolate ice cream with a white plastic spoon while drinking coffee at the local diner. We soon discover that Hank is the foreman of the squad that will execute Lawrence Musgrove for killing a cop. This is the reason for his sleeplessness and vomiting. Hank tells Sonny, who will be a part of the "strapdown team" for the first time, "You can't think about what you did or anything else about it. It's a job, and we have to do our job right." But Hank is unable to follow his own advice. *"You work and worry your way through life, and what do you have to show for it? As long as you live, everything you do brings nothing but worry and heartache. Even at night your mind can't rest. It is all useless" (2:22–23).*

The second family we meet in the movie is the Musgroves. As *Monster's Ball* opens, Lawrence (Sean Combs) is about to die in the electric chair for killing a cop. His wife, Leticia, has come to the penitentiary with their son, Tyrell (Coronji Calhoun), for a last visit. As with our introduction to the Grotowskis, the scene is shot so as to highlight the distance and isolation. Tyrell, who idolizes his dad, tells him that his drawing of him sitting in jail alone has been chosen in a contest for his school magazine's cover. "The theme," Leticia adds, "was solitude." Leticia goes on to tell her husband that her car is leaking and she can't keep up the payments on the house. With Tyrell looking out the window, she also tells Lawrence that the only reason she is there is "so you can say good-bye to your son." After eleven years of coming to the prison, she says, "I'm tired." *"Everything leads to weariness—a weariness too great for words" (1:8).*

Soon Leticia and Tyrell are home waiting for the final phone call that doesn't come. She escapes by drinking miniature bottles of Jack Daniels. Tyrell, who is obese, sneaks chocolate candy bars, even after his mom in frustration hits him and reduces him to tears by calling him "a fat little piggy." Ironically (and perhaps heavy-handedly), the TV they are watching switches to an advertisement for ReMax realtors, which begins, "Starting to feel a little cramped by your present surroundings? Maybe it's time to expand your horizons." *"So life came to mean nothing to me, because everything in it had brought me nothing but trouble. It had all been useless; I had been chasing the wind" (2:17).*

Leticia's world is filled with randomness, injustice, and hatred. In the words of Qoheleth, she lives her life *"in darkness and grief, worried, angry, and sick" (5:17).* With her husband on death row, she must raise her son as a single mom. Car breakdowns, eviction notices, job terminations, racial taunts, and her son's death threaten to rob her life of any semblance of meaning. Just before the hit-and-run killing of her son, we see a man walking by the side of the road carrying a sandwich board with the message (again somewhat too obviously), "It's got to be somebody's fault." But that is just the point. It is everyone's fault and no one's fault. The world is what it is. *"The longer you argue, the more useless it is, and you are no better off" (6:11).* As Lawrence is going to the electric chair, the scene cuts to Leticia's house, where she is seen in the bathroom brushing her teeth. She would love to get the taste of these past eleven years out of her mouth, but she cannot. *"Then I looked again at all the injustice that goes on in this world. The oppressed were crying, and no one would help them. No one would help them, because their oppressors had power on their side" (4:1).*

Hank's world is little better than Leticia's. His father, Buck, might say to him, "We're family," but the words are like all the others, a mere pretense for control, devoid of feeling. After being humiliated by Hank for throwing up at Lawrence Musgrove's execution, Sonny confronts Hank: "You hate me. You hate me, don't you?" There is a pause, and then we hear Hank's unthinkable words: "Yeah, I hate you. I always did." Sonny can barely respond, "Well, I always loved you," before taking the gun he is holding and fatally shooting himself. Things are only made worse at the funeral, when Buck's one comment about his grandson is, "He was weak." Here are three lonely individuals incapable of familial relationship. *"If it is cold, two can sleep together and stay warm, but how can you keep warm by yourself?" (4:11).*

What is apparent is the endless cycle of meaninglessness and grief that characterizes the lives of these two families. Nothing seems to happen only once. We discover that suicide claimed the life of not only Hank's son but also his mother. Sonny's gravestone is next to those of both Hank's and Buck's wives in the backyard. We see Hank cleaning blood off naugahyde upholstery twice—once that of his son and once that of Leticia's son, Tyrell. But death refuses to be sanitized. There are three killings and three occasions when people throw up. Tyrell finds what little comfort he can by eating chocolate. Hank's solace is chocolate ice cream. Both Hank and Sonny go to the same prostitute, Vera, for passionless sex using an identical position. Hank abuses his son, as does Leticia. Tyrell is an artist, like Lawrence, his father. The long walk that Hank takes with Lawrence to the electric chair is mirrored in the long walk down the hall with his father, Buck, as Hank puts him in a nursing home. The repetitions go on and on. *"You spend your life*

Hank Grotowski (Billy Bob Thornton) and Leticia Musgrove (Halle Berry) in *Monster's Ball* (d. Forster, 2001). Photo by Jeanne Louise Bulliard. © 1999 Lions Gate Films. All rights reserved.

working, laboring, and what do you have to show for it? Generations come and generations go, but the world stays just the same. . . . What has happened before will happen again. What has been done before will be done again. There is nothing new in the whole world" (1:3–4, 9; cf. 3:15).

Such repetitions call into question all else in life, as does the recurring presence of death itself. You can't escape it. The movie's title, *Monster's Ball,* refers to the party that is sometimes thrown by the executioners the night before a killing. Here is a metaphor for life itself. We are on the road to death. The best there is, it might seem, is a final party. The execution sets the tone for all that happens in the film, and the subsequent deaths of Sonny and Tyrell only confirm death's ubiquity. Hank has tried to sanitize death's curse by doing his job on the execution squad emotionlessly and efficiently. When the boys are killed, first Sonny and later Tyrell, he twice tries to wash the bloodstains off the naugahyde. Lest he grieve, he even locks up his son's room. And when the minister at Sonny's funeral asks Hank if there is a passage from the Bible he wants read, Hank responds, "No, all I want to hear is that dirt hittin' that box." *"A human being is no better off than an animal, because life has no meaning for either. They are both going to the same place—the dust" (3:19–20).*

Learning to Enjoy the Present Moment

> Someone who is always thinking about happiness is a fool. A wise person thinks about death.
>
> Ecclesiastes 7:4

Death will not be denied . . . thankfully. In *Monster's Ball,* as in life itself, death provides the opportunity for a new awareness of life. Early in the movie, for example, we observe Lawrence Musgrove preparing to die. He has come to terms with who he is and seeks to reach out the best he can to those he is with. To Tyrell, his son, he says, "I'm a bad man. . . . But I want you to know something. . . . You ain't me." Tyrell, who loves his dad, responds, "Yes, I am." "No,"

says Lawrence, "you're not. You're everything that's good about me.
. . . You're the best of what I am."*

Back in his cell, Lawrence draws a picture of Sonny, who is
guarding him, and then offers the portrait to Sonny as a gift. Sonny
is deeply moved and reaches out through the bars to touch the
condemned man, who is having trouble breathing. When Hank
sees his son's emotion, he commands Sonny to sit down, but it is
too late. They have already connected as persons; the executioner is
no longer just a functionary. We see Sonny wiping his eyes. When
Lawrence turns to draw Hank, he tells both father and son, "I've
always believed that a portrait captures a person far better than a
photograph. It truly takes a human being to really see a human
being." Hank can only respond with a blank stare. But Sonny,
having seen Lawrence in a new light, throws up as he walks the
condemned man to the electric chair. Life's absurdity has been given
a visceral metaphor. *"Vanity of vanities, says the Teacher, vanity of
vanities! All is vanity" (1:2 NRSV).*

Sonny's awareness of his "life lived out in the midst of death"
comes early in the movie, mediated through the touch of a death
row inmate. For Hank to connect with his life takes much longer—and two more deaths—but it does come. The chief agent of
that revelation is Leticia. Hank's growth into human awareness is
painfully slow and halting—at times almost imperceptible given
his taciturn and silent demeanor. Though his colleagues try to quiet
his hateful tirade against his son by screaming, "This is not you,
Hank," Hank seems closer to the mark in his rejoinder, "This is
me." But the death of his son eventually forces him to reexamine
himself, and the picture is not pretty. He sees too much of his own
father, Buck, in himself.

Soon we see Hank driving to the penitentiary in the rain to turn in
his badge. He is framed on the screen so as to emphasize his feelings of
imprisonment and isolation. The music playing in the background has
been stretched and bent, reinforcing the slow agony of the situation.

---

*To emphasize Lawrence's hard-won peace, the filmmakers always shot him in
the center of the screen, while the characters with him are always situated on the
screen's edge.

"I quit the team," he later tells his dad, only for his dad to respond, "That was a mistake. . . . You're reminding me of your mother. . . . That woman failed me. . . . She quit on me. You're doing the same." Buck, in one sense, is right. Hank has quit on him. *"Nothing that I had worked for and earned meant a thing to me" (2:18)*. Despite his attempts to block it out, Hank has let his son's death teach him something about life. *"Sorrow is better than laughter; it may sadden your face, but it sharpens your understanding" (7:3)*.

And the lessons continue. Hank sees Leticia, the waitress who has served him coffee and ice cream at the diner, sobbing by the side of the road. Stopping to help, he discovers her holding the broken body of her son, who has been hit by a car. What at the beginning of the movie would have been unimaginable now happens. He reaches out to a black woman. As they drive to the hospital, Hank is clearly uncomfortable, but he stays at the hospital to give the police his account and, after cleaning the blood off Leticia's purse, even takes her home when asked to do so by the cop. For the second time, Hank has to clean blood off a vinyl seat. But while the stain comes off the backseat of his car, it has left an indelible mark on his conscience. *"It is better to go to a home where there is mourning than to one where there is a party, because the living should always remind themselves that death is waiting for us all" (7:2)*.

The next morning Hank stops his car to offer Leticia a ride to work. At the diner, rather than leaving an eight-cent tip like the last time, he leaves two dollars. Later that evening Hank returns to the diner for his chocolate ice cream and coffee and again offers Leticia a ride home. As they sit in the front seat of his car, each hugging their respective doors as if fearful to get any closer, Leticia asks Hank why he chose to help her. Hank, for the first time, allows another into his world. In slow and halting speech, he tells her:

> I don't know . . . doin' the right thing I guess. My son died. . . . I never was a very good father. . . . He's a good kid. . . . When I seen what you was going through there, it just made me think about somethin' . . . reminded me of somethin', I don't know. You know

when you feel like you can't breathe . . . you can't get out from inside yourself, really.*

Leticia invites Hank into her small house, where they seek relief by getting drunk on Jack Daniels. Still quiet and somber and clearly ill at ease, Hank tries to converse awkwardly but is brought up short when Leticia shows him drawings that her husband, Lawrence, had made. Although Hank realizes who she is, Leticia has no idea of their macabre connection. She can only continue to pour out her grief over the deaths in her family. Leticia keeps dropping her hand into Hank's lap without realizing it, but Hank is also unaware. Neither is relating to the other out of sexual attraction but out of shared grief and pain.

Hank finally says to her, "I'm not sure what you want me to do." It is only when Leticia responds from a deep inner recess of her being ("I want you to make me feel better. . . . I want you to make me feel good. . . . Can you make me feel good?") that their sexual urges come to the surface and the two make love in an orgy of primal need. The scene is raw, as is the emotion that causes it. "I needed you so much," Leticia says as they fall asleep in each other's arms. *"If it is cold, two can sleep together and stay warm, but how can you keep warm by yourself?" (4:11).*

Hank has connected emotionally with another person for the first time in years, and just as with Sonny, his reaction proves visceral. The pain is too much for him physically to take. In the morning as he looks at a picture of Lawrence, which Leticia has hung in her bathroom, Hank throws up. But also as with Sonny, Hank's sickness is an ironic indicator of his growing health—it is both symbolically and actually an attempt to expurgate the bile that has characterized his life.

Soon Hank takes his son's truck to his black neighbor and asks him to get it ready to sell. In actuality, he is going to give it to

---

*It is left unclear whether Tyrell might have actually walked out on the highway because he was despondent over his father's death and his mother's verbal abuse. Hank and Leticia might have this in common too: pushing their children over the edge emotionally by their constant berating.

Leticia. Leticia has her own gift for Hank, but in yet another cruel twist, Hank is gone when she arrives to give him the present, and she must, instead, endure the crude racial and sexual slurs of his father. Once again doubting the genuineness of their relationship, Leticia takes her anger out on the returning Hank and roars out of the driveway, gravel flying.

Hank has now changed, however; he will not be deterred. He checks his father into a nursing home, despite his protests. We sense that if Hank doesn't sever this relationship immediately, he will be doomed to the same fate. "I don't wanna go out like this," Buck tells Hank. "Neither do I," is Hank's matter-of-fact reply. After leaving the nursing home, Hank returns home and begins to paint his house a lighter color. He purchases a gas station and names it "Leticia's." "Who is Leticia?" a neighbor asks. "My girlfriend," Hank replies. There will be a new day.

Unfortunately, there are still more twists to the story. Darkness and grief continue to intrude. Leticia is evicted from her house, and Hank must take her to his/their new home. In a scene with almost no dialogue that lasts over five minutes, Hank shows Leticia his house. He offers to sleep in another room if that would make her more comfortable, but Leticia has forgiven him. Their previously raw passion based in loneliness and need now gives way to tender kisses. They are almost shy with each other. They smile and laugh together as Hank focuses his attention on how he can make Leticia happy.* "That felt good?" he asks her when they are through. "Yeah," is her simple reply.

When Hank goes out to buy some ice cream, Leticia, alone in the house, discovers in a box the pictures Lawrence had drawn of Hank and Sonny. The cruelty of life seems to have no limits. *"Like birds suddenly caught in a trap, like fish caught in a net, we are trapped at some evil moment when we least expect it"* (9:12). All the emotion of her former life floods back on her as she realizes the bitter truth. Confusion. Anger. Disappointment. She finally breaks down weeping.

---

*The fact that the focus is on how the man can make the woman happy, not vice versa, makes this love scene atypical in Hollywood portrayals.

Rather than give viewers the obligatory confrontation (and then perhaps reconciliation) scene that Hollywood is so good at, the filmmakers refrain, allowing the ambiguity of life to have, instead, its final say. On the way home from the store, Hank drives by the gas station he has purchased—Leticia's name is painted on its sign. When he gets home, Leticia seems dazed. "Are you okay?" he asks. She can only nod slowly. In silence they go outside and sit on the steps. Viewers see Leticia struggling with her conflicting emotions. She looks out in the backyard where Sonny and the two Grotowski women are buried. Perhaps she realizes that too many people have already died. Perhaps she senses that both she and Hank are similar in the grief and loss they have experienced. Hank feeds her a spoon of chocolate ice cream, and she accepts it. After an extended silence, Hank says, "I went by *our* station on the way home. . . . I like *our* sign. . . . I think *we're* going to be all right" (emphasis added). In the background, the music, which has been supporting the growing tension, resolves into a small melody. There is hope even for the flawed and the needful. *"Two people can resist an attack that would defeat one person alone" (4:12).*

Is Joy Enough?
What about Redemption?

Critics have sometimes mistakenly considered *Monster's Ball* a tale of "interracial redemption."[3] Moira Macdonald of the *Seattle Times,* for example, says that the movie gives us "a low-key gift of redemption and love."[4] Even the director echoes this hope. But isn't this claim too much for an ending shot through with ambiguity? In the movie, as in life, such meaning is denied us. Life remains inscrutable and too often unjust. The inevitable arrival of death awaits us all. The two characters have only the present moment and its joy, but it is enough. And we hope against hope that it will continue for a season more.

We do not know why Leticia chooses not to confront Hank. Is it because of the gravestones that she sees? Is death now being put to the service of life? Or does she sense why Hank might have kept this last information from her? Did he have a choice? Does she sense his love? Does she forgive? Or is she just too tired to scream? What are her alternatives? Perhaps it is a mixture of all the above. The movie does not provide clear answers to life's mysteries. It is enough for now to enjoy the ice cream and the care that accompanies it. It is enough to hear the melody and know that joy is for the moment possible:

> But anyone who is alive in the world of the living has some hope; a live dog is better off than a dead lion. Yes, the living know they are going to die, but the dead know nothing. They have no further reward; they are completely forgotten. Their loves, their hates, their passions, all died with them. They will never again take part in anything that happens in this world.
>
> Go ahead—eat your food and be happy; drink your wine and be cheerful. It's all right with God. . . . Enjoy life with the one you love, as long as you live the useless life that God has given you in this world. Enjoy every useless day of it, because that is all you will get for all your trouble.
>
> 9:4–9

Many have failed to understand this chastened yet positive advice from Qoheleth. Isn't it cynically hedonistic, something like what Siduri offers Gilgamesh: "Eat, drink, and be merry, for tomorrow we die"? No, while death is ever present, as the gravestones remind them, it is denied final claim. For others, Ecclesiastes' words seem ludicrous, a cynical sop, given our harsh and amoral world. But for Hank and Leticia, however modest their present joy, it is enough. It rings true to their experience, and it is real joy. Pleasure cannot be sought blindly but only with the full awareness of life's harshness and mystery. The two wounded lovers might not have any ultimate answers. The personal flaws and social ills that define their existences will no doubt remain. But *"two are better off than one, because together they can work more effectively. If one of them falls down, the other can help him up. . . . If it is cold, two can sleep together and stay warm.*

. . . Two people can resist an attack that would defeat one person alone"
(4:9–12). And the ice cream is good!

Life's monstrous deceits and half measures need purging, a purging beyond anything the story can provide. Although we cheer as Buck is taken to the nursing home, this is but a start. Nevertheless, something more than life's alienation and desperation is now available. What Norbert Lohfink recognizes in Qoheleth might also be said of *Monster's Ball:* "Everything is shot through not merely with melancholy, but also with a modest, yet never-failing delight in the happiness which is nevertheless given to man. Qoheleth seeks to guide man into a joyful existence before the face of death, which he never forgets."[5]

Karl Barth listened daily to Mozart, finding in his music a joy that "overtakes sorrow without extinguishing it, in which the Yea rings louder than the ever-present Nay."[6] Barth wrote often about his fondness for Mozart, for the rootedness that he discovered there. His observation concerning Mozart seems relevant here:

> He [Mozart] had heard the harmony of creation to which the shadow also belongs but in which the shadow is not darkness, deficiency is not defeat, sadness cannot become despair, trouble cannot degenerate into tragedy and infinite melancholy is not ultimately forced to claim undisputed sway. . . . The light shines all the more brightly because it breaks forth from the shadow. The sweetness is also bitter and cannot therefore cloy. Life does not fear death, but knows it well.[7]

Here is an analogue of *Monster's Ball.*

7

CAN GOD BE IN THIS?

M. Night Shyamalan and *Signs*

God is interested in a lot of things besides Religion. God is the Lord and Creator of all life, and there are manifestations of the holy in its celebration or its repudiation—in every aspect of the common life.

Joseph Sittler, *Gravity and Grace*

All of us struggle, at some point in our lives, with our fears of the unknown and our experiences of life's injustices. More particularly, all of us are caught short by the reality of death, our own or that of one close to us. The preceding chapters provide more than ample evidence that life is incredibly messy; at times it seems almost more than we can bear. When life's circumstances close in on us in this way, there are two responses we might take, or so suggests Graham Hess (Mel Gibson), the Pennsylvania minister in M. Night Shyamalan's *Signs*. Graham abandoned his calling after his wife's senseless death. As he and his brother, Merrill (Joaquin

Phoenix), now sit glued to the television set watching a live feed from Mexico City documenting signs of an alien invasion in the form of bright lights in the sky, Merrill asks his older brother if this could be the end of the world. With no emotion or empathy, Graham responds, "Yes." This leads Merrill to challenge Graham, "Can you pretend to be like you used to be? Give me some comfort."

This nonpracticing cleric, who has experienced both sides of the faith equation, proceeds to give Merrill a twofold typology of how people respond to tragedy and/or injustice. He tells his brother:

> People break down into two groups. When they experience something lucky, group number one sees it as more than luck, more than coincidence. They see it as a sign, evidence that there is someone up there watching out for them. Group number two sees it as just pure luck, a happy turn of chance.
>
> Oh, sure, the people in group number two are looking at those fourteen lights in a very suspicious way. For them, this situation isn't 50/50. It could be bad, it could be good. But deep down they feel that whatever happens, they're on their own. And that fills them with fear. . . .
>
> But there's a whole lot of people in group number one, and they see those fourteen lights. They're looking at a miracle. And deep down they feel that whatever is going to happen, there'll be someone there to help them. And that fills them with hope. . . .
>
> You have to ask yourself . . . what kind of person are you? Are you the kind that sees signs, sees miracles, or do you believe that people just get lucky? Or look at the question this way, is it possible that there are no coincidences?

Merrill, a former minor league baseball player, is portrayed as having neither brains nor direction in life. Yet he has come to live with his older brother, Graham, to help him and his two young children cope with the death of their wife and mother. He relieves the growing tension by immediately giving a ludicrous example of how he was distracted at a party just as he was to kiss a girl who seconds later threw up all over herself. "I knew the second it happened it was a miracle. I could have been kissing her when she threw up." Chuckling out loud, he pronounces to his brother, "I'm a miracle man. These lights are a miracle." But as an audience we know, as do these brothers, that the answer to this question is too important to be decided so lightly.

A comparable question has been weaving itself through many of the pages of this book, a question also central to the writer of Ecclesiastes. Where is God in the evil and tragedy of life? Could God be present even here, or is this but cruel fate, circumstance, blind luck? In *American Beauty*, Ricky, while watching a plastic bag dancing in the air, apprehends that "there was this entire life behind things, and this incredibly benevolent force that wanted me to know there was no reason to be afraid . . . ever." Despite his abusive circumstance—or better, given his circumstances—he confesses that there is at times "almost too much beauty," something Lester also comes to realize in the moments just before his death.

Similarly, in *Run Lola Run,* blind chance again gives way to fate's gracious intention. Lola lives into her destiny as she abandons any attempt to solve life's crises by her own efforts and instead utters an inchoate prayer for help, one not tied to a particular religious tradition but spiritual in its intention nonetheless. For the director Tom Tykwer, our lives are graciously supported by a larger spiritual presence. Though life may look as chaotic as the thousands of people milling around in the field at the movie's opening, nothing is without significance. There is divine meaning and purpose to our activity. As already noted, when viewed "from above," the people in the field spell out the movie's title, *Lola Rennt.*

In *Magnolia,* the narrator of the audacious prologue is Ricky Jay, who in real life hosts a TV show about bizarre yet true events. He sets the interpretive parameters for the story that follows, stating, "And it is the humble opinion of this narrator that this is not just something that happened. This cannot be 'one of those things.' This, please, cannot be that. . . . This was not just a matter of chance. . . . These strange things happen all the time." Television might provide perspective for our traditional human agendas of pleasure, fame, and knowledge (though it is often as unreliable as the weather forecasts that dot the movie), but such wisdom proves inadequate to handle life's biggest mysteries—certainly inadequate for the frogs that fall from the sky at the movie's end. There is no explicit reference to God in the movie, but the repeated Exodus references as well as the frogs themselves suggest that we have witnessed a supernatural intervention, an offer to "wise up" and realize the futility of trying to "save" one's self. The gift of life must come from another (an Other?).

This same faint but real spiritual presence will also be seen in *About Schmidt* (see chap. 8). Again, the context for the writer-director's proffered wisdom is life's messiness—the seeming futility of our work, our effort. Warren Schmidt's job, marriage, and family are taken from him. For most of the movie he either denies this stark reality or assumes life's trauma to be everyone else's fault. But as he realizes both his need for others and his own complicity in life's disappointments, he begins to accept his own responsibility for his life. Sitting on the roof of his RV with candles lit, he even asks his dead wife, Helen, for forgiveness for letting her down. As he does, a shooting star streaks across the sky, and Warren instinctively makes the sign of the cross. His confession is a holy moment. At its core, life has a spiritual center.

Such a core, spiritual truth is also central to *Monster's Ball,* though there is no hint of a divine presence. "Spirit" (capital "S") has simply become "spirit." As the movie ends, Leticia and Hank have found solace in the presence ("present") of each other given life's brutal circumstances. We cannot save ourselves from life's injustice, mystery, and death, but grace can be found in another. We can share life's pain with another and in that find peace.

This litany of spirit and Spirit may seem forced to some and insufficient to others. What signs are present in this messy world that there really is a divine power graciously turned toward us? Why call it God? Isn't God present in other and more direct ways? How can we ever link God and evil circumstance? Why would we want to? The Christian or the Jew may ask, "Hasn't God revealed himself to be our gracious God in salvation's history?" Questions from both those with faith and those lacking it would seem to drown out the quiet music of the Spirit. But do they? It is questions such as these that M. Night Shyamalan addresses in his movie *Signs* (2002).

A Sci-Fi Thriller, a Family Drama, a Narrative of Faith?

The movie *Signs* is actually three stories interwoven into one, each supplying a different component of the larger narrative. The first, a tale of an alien invasion, anchors the movie's plot. It involves crop circles and things that go bump in the night. Ultimately, this is the least important of the three stories, though it is the hook that grabs viewers initially. The second, a heartwarming drama of a grieving family trying to cope with the loss of their wife and mother, provides insight into the narrative's characters. In the process, it gives the film its heart. We come to know and care about the Hesses, particularly the children. The third, the story of a clergyman's recovery of faith, reveals Shyamalan's belief that all that happens, all life's seeming coincidences, fit into a larger divinely ordered pattern, one graciously directed toward humanity's well-being. This third story challenges us to consider our own beliefs concerning what reality is like beneath the vicissitudes of life. This third story, rooted in what is unalterable about life, is ultimately the soul of the film. For its spirituality to have power or meaning, however, we must first engage the other stories.

Story 1: An Alien Invasion

Signs tells the tale of an alien invasion, much like those cult classics of the 1950s and 1960s, *Invasion of the Body Snatchers* and *Night of the Living Dead.* Unlike *Independence Day* and other more contemporary movies that are long on pyrotechnics and graphic horror but short on suspense and story, *Signs* functions according to the premise that less is more. With a conscious tip of the hat to Alfred Hitchcock's *The Birds* (1963), the movie illustrates that what we imagine often proves scarier than what is actually shown to us. Viewers strain to see what is thought to be in the field or behind the door. Using long shots to invite viewers to wonder what it is they are really looking at, then punctuating their growing anxiety with sudden partial shocks (a shadow, a fleeting foot, a groping hand), Shyamalan creates a claustrophobic nightmare that builds in suspense.

The movie opens as Graham awakens with a fright, having heard weird calls and noises. Graham looks out into his backyard through a window distorted by warps in the pane of glass, sensing that something is amiss. In the background, John Newton Howard's music, played by violins, increases the expectation that something is not right. Grabbing his brother, Merrill, Graham runs out into his cornfield in search of his children, whom they have heard calling. When they find Bo (Abigail Breslin), she asks her father if he is part of her dream. Then, finding his young son, Morgan (Rory Culkin), Graham is informed by the boy, "I think God did it." Graham turns to discover a huge crop circle in his field. A large section of his crop has been bent to the ground without the stalks being broken. As the camera cuts to a shot from above, we see a series of such circles and lines in his field making strange geometric shapes.

Graham, of course, rejects his son's "naive" conjecture about a divine cause, choosing to believe in something more logical. It must be a prank by his juvenile delinquent neighbor boys. But answers are not so easily forthcoming. Instead, life presents itself as increasingly out of kilter. The children tell their father that the dog has peed on the kitchen floor. Bo, the five-year-old daughter, believes her water is contaminated. Their dog growls viciously. By the time Caroline (Cherry Jones), the local police woman, informs Graham that other animals in the area are also acting funny, some of them even violent ("It's almost like they act when they smell a predator around, peeing on themselves and everything."), we are hooked.

And so the story builds. Who or what are these aliens? Are they friendly or hostile? Will this story be more like *Close Encounters* or *Independence Day*? Events unfold like a nightmare, and with every new revelation, our anxiety mounts. *"The wiser you are, the more worries you have; the more you know, the more it hurts" (1:18)*. And thus it is for Graham. Breaking news on all the television stations describes how similar crop circles, "signs," are showing up around the world. Later, TV reporters tell viewers that there are lights in the sky over major cities. "Extraterrestrials," says Morgan. But again, the adults are not yet ready to believe.

Graham Hess (Mel Gibson); his son, Morgan (Rory Culkin); and his daughter, Bo (Abigail Breslin); together with Graham's brother, Merrill (Joaquin Phoenix), investigate strange occurrences on their farm. *Signs* (d. Shyamalan, 2002). Photo by Frank Masi. © 2002 Touchtone Pictures. All rights reserved.

Throughout the story, Shyamalan momentarily relieves the mounting tension through the use of humor, only to bring viewers back to the terror with new intensity. We see, for example, the kids putting tin foil helmets on their heads so the aliens can't read their minds. But immediately, Graham is called over to his neighbor's house, where he finds an alien locked in the pantry. Graham is able to escape an attack by the alien's hand reaching under the door by slicing off two of its fingers. Viewers temporarily breathe a sigh of relief when the Hess family barricades themselves in their basement for protection, but we know they will ultimately need to fight for their lives.

Story 2: A Family in Turmoil

Although *Signs* can be criticized for its anticlimatic final showdown and for the surprise revelation that makes victory possible, these matters are somewhat beside the point, for by then, the movie's focus has turned to other matters. Initially concerned about the aliens, viewers find themselves increasingly anxious about a family that has been thrown into personal crisis. In this way, *Signs* proves to be not only scary but also tender.* As Peter Travers of *Rolling Stone* says so well in his review, Shyamalan "turns the goose-pimple genre on its empty head and fills it with spirit, purpose and emotionally bruised characters who add up to more than body count."[1]

We empathize with each of the four members of the Hess family as the movie unfolds as a family drama. The horror story gives the movie a necessary edge, keeping its sweetness from degenerating into a maudlin sentimentality. Yet it is not the mystery of the extraordinary that ultimately snares us; it is the sanctity of the ordinary. As we watch Graham hold his son during an asthma attack brought on by the young boy's fear, this father is not the only one trying to breathe air into the lungs of the child. As viewers, we too cry out for relief. There has been too much grief already in this family.

Shyamalan's commitment to the family is sincerely held. He has a close, even dependent relationship with his extended family. He lives not five minutes from his parents in a Philadelphia suburb. A cover story that ran in *Newsweek* at the time of the opening of *Signs* highlighted the sense of security and meaning that his relationship with his family has brought him. It is not surprising, then, to find that these same themes are woven into the fabric of his movies. In two of the most tender moments of the story, the writer-director has Graham trying to calm down his children by sharing with them the stories of their births. The stories told on the screen are, in fact, the real stories of the births of Shyamalan's own two children. The felt authenticity of the descriptions simply adds to their vicarious impact. As Jeff Giles writes, "Like all of Shyamalan's movies, *Signs* is obsessed not just with the unknown, but with family . . . and shot through with the unmistakable admonition that we must draw whoever is near and dear to us even nearer.[2]

---

*It is worth noting that initially the largest groups of fans that turned out for *The Sixth Sense* were young boys and older women. For the one, the suspense captured their imagination. For the other, it was the human relationships, the pathos of a family coping with crisis. Here again, Shyamalan combines two factors, fear and family.

Within the first ten minutes of the movie, we are introduced
to the main characters: Graham; his children, Bo and Morgan;
and his brother, Merrill. Missing, obviously, is the mother of this
family. It takes the whole of the movie for us to learn more fully
about this single-parent family, but we soon realize that Graham
and his children are trying to cope with the recent traumatic loss
of their wife and mother, Colleen. There is an intimacy in their
portrayals, despite the fact that Graham has in defense shut down
much of his emotion.

As the story proceeds, Shyamalan uses two devices to usher us
into their lives. The first takes place when Caroline, the investigating
police officer, encourages Graham to take his family into town to
get their minds back on everyday things. As they each wander off in
their own directions in the small town, the people they encounter
provide background information. Merrill stops at the army recruiting
office. It turns out he has several minor league records for home runs,
but he has also struck out so often that no team now wants him.
The children go into a bookstore to find a book on extraterrestrials.
When Bo is given a glass of water and she rejects it as "contaminated,"
Morgan explains to the perplexed owners, "It's like a tick people
have, except it's not a tick." Throughout the story, Bo leaves water
glasses sitting around the house, given this phobia. It is endearing
(and, as it turns out, crucial for the surprise ending). In one of the
funniest scenes of the movie, Graham goes into the pharmacy to get
medicine for Morgan's asthma. Tracy, the clerk, calls him Father and
wants to say confession to him. Though Graham tells her he is not
a reverend anymore ("haven't been for six months"), she goes right
ahead. Given the ominous events reported over the store's radio, she
feels the need to clear her conscience.

Second, to keep some suspense present as to why Graham has
rejected his calling, Shyamalan splices into several segments a flashback of the accident in which Colleen was crushed between Ray
Reddy's truck and a tree. Ray has told Graham apologetically, "It was
like it was meant to be," but Graham rejects such fatalism. As we
watch him relive in his mind the crash and its aftermath, we come
to understand his bitterness toward God. The crash seems to reveal
the absence of any larger meaning, any higher power, that could

make sense of such nonsense. *"I used my wisdom to test all of this. I was determined to be wise, but it was beyond me. How can anyone discover what life means?" (7:23–24).* His wife's ludicrous final words to him, telling Merrill to "swing away," seem to Graham the final straw. *"It isn't right! We go just as we came. We labor, trying to catch the wind, and what do we get? We get to live our lives in darkness and grief, worried, angry, and sick" (5:16).*

Story 3: A God Who Is Present

While an obvious love exists between the members of the Hess family, they also experience a deepening tension as the story unfolds. Graham seems able to deal with only surface reality—his farm, his son's asthma, his daughter's obsession with water, Merrill's failures as a ball player. The family, however, needs more from their father than this. Merrill has looked to his brother for inspiration, but now Graham has become the problem. As Merrill tells his brother, there are things he can take and some things he can't: "One of them I can't take is when my older brother, who is everything I want to be, starts losing faith in things."

This subtext to the family drama, the need for Graham to recover his religious belief, becomes the movie's third story line. Here is where the real power and meaning of the narrative reside, for rather than being plot driven or character centered, this story is ultimately controlled by its God-hauntedness. It is this sense of divine mystery over against which both plot and characterization play out. *"God made everything, and you can no more understand what he does than you understand how new life begins in the womb of a pregnant woman" (11:5).* The absence and the presence of the divine for Graham ultimately drive this story forward.

The children still live in the God-shaped world of their father's former calling. *"After all this, there is only one thing to say: Have reverence for God, and obey his commands, because this is all that we were created for" (12:13).* Similarly, the crisis brought on by the alien invasion has caused the townspeople to turn in fear to consider their relationship with God. Even the TV newscaster reports that hundreds of thousands of people are flocking to temples, synagogues, and churches. The anchorman concludes his broadcast by saying, "God be with us all." *"No matter how much you dream, how much useless work you do, or how much you talk, you must still stand in awe of God" (5:7).*

Graham Hess, however, will have none of this. As he sits down with his family for what might be their last supper (each, like on death row, has picked his or her favorite comfort food), the children wait with bowed heads for their father to pray. "What's the matter with everyone?" Graham asks. "Maybe we should say a prayer," is Morgan's response. When his father refuses angrily, Morgan lashes out, "I hate you. You let Mom die." The scene degenerates as Graham tries to will his family into enjoying the meal, until Morgan finally comes and hugs his father. All four end up hugging one another in their grief. *"Two people can resist an attack that would defeat one person alone. A rope of three cords is hard to break" (4:12).*

The moment at the dinner table proves paradigmatic. Soon Graham is locked in the basement with his family for protection from the aliens, holding his asthmatic son in his arms. Fearing for his son's life, Graham yells at God, using the same words his son used: "I hate you. Don't do this to me again. Not again." *"Look at what happens in the world: sometimes the righteous get the punishment of the wicked, and the wicked get the reward of the righteous. I say it is useless" (8:14).* Though Graham is angry with God, he has had to admit the divine back into his reality. *"God sends both happiness and trouble; you never know what is going to happen next" (7:14).* Here is Graham's first step back toward faith.

Realizing that fear, by causing the asthma attack, is actually killing his son, Graham tells Morgan, "Don't be afraid of what is happening. . . . Believe it is going to pass . . . believe it . . . don't be afraid . . . believe . . . we don't have to be afraid." Viewers sense that his advice has more than one intended target. In the final, surprising denouement, Graham realizes that the random circumstances surrounding his wife's death contain clues necessary to repel the attacker. "Swing away" takes on new meaning. So too does Bo's phobia about water. His son's asthma, rather than being life threatening, actually proves life giving, as it keeps the alien's poisonous gas from entering his lungs. *"Everything that happens in this world happens at the time God chooses" (3:1)*. Overcome by the realization that life's "coincidences" seem to fit into a larger pattern, Graham responds to his son's question, "Did someone save me?" by affirming, "I think someone did." *"One thing God does is to make us stand in awe of him" (3:14)*.

The movie's closing mirrors its idyllic opening. We look out on a perfect backyard with a swing and crops in the corner, but this time the window glass is clear. There is no warp. As the music crescendos, it is now winter. Hess, the father, has again become Father Hess. It is Sunday, and we see him in his collar getting ready for church. The movie ends with the sound of children's laughter.

Signs is ultimately about those markers, or signs, that allow Graham to recover his faith. It is not merely about crop circles. Despite circumstances—or better, within circumstances—Graham recovers his belief that, as the hymn writer penned, "This is my Father's world." "And though the wrong seems oft so strong, God is the ruler yet."[3] In the movie, Shyamalan uses a series of symbols to reinforce this belief. (Here is yet a third meaning for signs.) From the opening credits on, the sun, moon, and stars are constantly present. We see them on the wind chimes, shutters, and curtains. A circle of light unifies the credits. Creation opens us to the Creator. But these classical symbols of spirituality do not best capture the movie's intention. That is done by the faint outline of a cross on Graham's bedroom wallpaper, a sad reminder of a faith once embraced. After his wife's death, Graham removed the actual cross from his house, but the sun had faded the wall, such that the cross's image remained indelibly present. Graham tried to excise the divine, but God's presence remained present nonetheless.

Meaning amid Life's Fragments

Sister Rose Pacatte has noted that, like Steven Spielberg, "Shyamalan leaves a footprint in his films." In support of her thesis, she mentions two recurring motifs in his movies: "grief for a loved one who has died and the search for understanding of what is seemingly inexplicable."[4] She is correct, but what identifies a "typical" Shyamalan film is broader than his portrayals of these constants in human experience that call into question even our best efforts. One finds in this writer-director's movies not only a struggle to make sense out of life, given its injustices and mystery, but also a commitment to look beneath life's commonsense, everyday explanations. There is also a belief in the importance of family, or relationships, as a safe harbor, given life's vicissitudes, and a deep interest in the supernatural, in what lies beyond human explanation that might prove liberating.

Each of these interests is embodied in *Signs*. It is not enough to say, as Merrill does to Morgan, "Morgan, this crop stuff is just about a bunch of nerds who never had a girlfriend in their lives. They're like thirty now. They make up secret codes and analyze Greek mythology and make secret societies where other guys who never had girlfriends can join in." We know, as Merrill knows, that such commonsense explanations fail to scratch the surface. We must learn to see anew.

Shyamalan's first studio release, *Wide Awake* (1998), a movie that he felt was compromised by a final studio recut, tells the story of a fifth-grade boy, Joshua Beal, who searches for proof of God's existence after his grandfather, whom he loved, dies of cancer. Josh's reason for the search is to find out whether his devoted and devout Catholic grandfather is okay. The story is structured around three segments: the questions, the signs, and the answers. The signs come in a series of small, quirky events (a surprise snowfall, a friend's new faith, a cryptic message). They help the young boy begin to see life through fresh eyes. Resolution finally occurs in a sudden intense awareness of the world's sorrow and beauty, Josh becoming "wide awake." "I spent this year looking for something," he says, "and ended up seeing everything around me. It's like I was asleep. I'm wide awake now."

In *The Sixth Sense* (1999), both Cole Sear (as in one who sees), an eight-year-old boy who sees the dead walking around like regular people, and Malcolm Crowe, the child psychologist who tries to help him but ends up being helped, can't sort out the meaning of their complicated lives, though they try. Cole obviously wants and needs help: "I see dead people. They want me to do things for them." And Crowe, having been shot by an ex-patient, has his own struggles. His wife, once close to him, seems disinterested in hearing him when he talks to her. Promoted rightly as a scary ghost story, the film is also a drama about relationships, in particular about the importance of family. The movie's shocking ending brings its two plotlines to a single conclusion, causing audiences worldwide to return to theaters or to rent DVDs for a second viewing to see what they had inexplicably overlooked. Not only the characters in the movie need to observe the signs more closely. We, the audience, experience the need to do so as well.

The Sixth Sense was a surprise hit, garnering six Academy Award nominations and almost $300 million in box office receipts in the United States alone. Scores who saw this thriller were challenged to admit to similar experiences when they too felt "the prickly things on the back of your neck." As the movie's composer, James Newton Howard, reflects on the DVD of *The Sixth Sense,* "I think for a lot of people, this was a religious experience, very much nothing short of a religious experience for people. . . . Once in a while

Haunted by a dark secret, eight-year-old Cole Sear (Haley Joel Osment) talks with child psychologist Malcom Crowe (Bruce Willis). *The Sixth Sense* (d. Shyamalan, 1999). Photo by Ron Phillips. © 1999 Spyglass Entertainment Group. All rights reserved.

cultural events occur that . . . provide people with opportunities to crystallize some of their own notions about what may happen after we all leave this planet."⁵ The movie's ability to invite in the sacred extended even to Shyamalan himself. He relates how the movie unexpectedly "opened on my birthday, August 6th, which was another sign that the movie was just in a weird place and [was] guided."⁶ A deep correlation exists between themes in the film and beliefs held dear by the director, and he invites us to join with him in having faith in what lies beyond human explanation.

In the movie *Unbreakable* (2001), starring Samuel L. Jackson and Bruce Willis, Shyamalan continues his exploration of what defies human explanation. David Dunn (Willis), a security guard, is the sole survivor of a horrible train crash. More incredible, he does not have a single scratch. The fact that David is "unbreakable" defies explanation. Through meeting up with a mysterious stranger (Jackson), one who believes that comic book heroes actually populate the earth, David is able to get in touch with and then accept the fact that, despite rational explanations to the contrary, he possesses superhuman abilities. In a fascinating commentary on the DVD, Shyamalan talks of trying to make a "feature-length *Twilight Zone*," where through a slight of hand or a flip of the plot, the commonsense trivialization of everyday life is overturned. Though the movie failed to become the cultural phenomenon that *The Sixth Sense* became, its continuing status as a cult favorite suggests he was largely successful in his intention.

Even from this brief overview, it should be apparent that Shyamalan's interests in the movie *Signs* are not unique to it. Rather, they take up and extend interests that have been consistent throughout his career.* He calls us to be wide awake to God's lurking presence. (His production company is even named Blinding Edge Pictures.) We need to hone our senses, to become aware of the signs that life provides, for given life's injustices and the finality of death itself, life's fragile spiritual presence too often remains unnoticed.

---

*Even the movie *Stuart Little*, for which Shyamalan wrote the screenplay, centers on the importance of family.

Shyamalan invites his viewers to have faith in what lies beyond all human possibility.

The Reception of *Signs*

Shyamalan started production on *Signs* the day after the terror of 9/11. He commented, "It was very difficult, difficult and meaningful. It made the metaphor of the movie more real for us. Everybody had lines that were ridiculously real for us. It was weird."[7] After the cast read through the complete script on 9/12, the production team held a candlelight vigil. Then the next morning, the first scene on the schedule was shot. It happened to be the horrific final conversation between Graham and Colleen, as she is fatally trapped between Ray's truck and a tree. The absurdity of life, given death, was all too real. The story's heightened meaning in light of 9/11 carried over even a year later, when viewers, still looking for what could bring hope in a continuing context of random evil and terror, made *Signs* another box office hit for Shyamalan.

One Australian critic mistakenly concluded after seeing the film that "*Signs* is not really about theology at all. It is about politics."[8] But this is not what the movie is about. The script does not include, for example, a military solution to the alien invasion, leaving viewers at the end vaguely unsettled about future terror that might still be lurking. Is the aliens' retreat temporary? We don't know, for the film's narrative has moved on to other important matters, issues of faith and doubt. As we enter with Graham and his family into their grief, as we experience unimaginable and life-threatening evil, we don't wonder about possible government solutions. Rather, we find ourselves asking the same questions that Merrill and Graham ask. Do we believe that even in the worst of circumstances there is a God who is in charge and is watching over us? Is this possible? Or do we think life is out of control, the result of random circumstances and blind chance? Is that possible?

The movie is theologically centered. As Jeffrey Overstreet perceptively wrote, Shyamalan "puts us in the middle of a nightmare and forces us to ask what kind of person we would be if we were there. And the end effect, for all the misfortune that befalls our characters, is ultimately uplifting and encouraging."[9]

Yet not all Christian film critics liked the movie. In his otherwise helpful article on the spiritual imagination of Shyamalan, Roy Anker questions the theological seriousness of this "God-haunted writer-director" who traffics in "ghosts, superheroes, angels-in-disguise, and mysterious deathbed providences" and who recognizes "how God might just show up in the strangest places doing the most peculiar things." In particular, Anker questions what he believes is the suggestion that God does evil. Surely here is "a minor and very dubious theological point."[10] Anker is hardly alone in questioning Shyamalan's religious perspective. The critic for the U.S. Conference of Catholic Bishops complained that in *Signs,* Shyamalan's treatment of faith is "superficial." Bob Smithouser of Focus on the Family questioned the movie's "ambiguous spirituality." And Ted Baehr in his *Movieguide* found in Shyamalan's film an unhelpful mixture of Hinduism and liberal Episcopalianism (though other Christian reviewers were quick to recognize that Shyamalan's denial of mere coincidence is actually consistent with Christian teaching).[11] Dick Staub concluded his review of *Signs* by opining, "One senses Shyamalan does not care so much about the specifics—He just wants us to believe."[12]

What are we to make of such criticism and caution from Christian quarters? Is Shyamalan's a belief in belief, a contentless fuzzy affirmation of a general spirituality? Is the portrayal of belief in *Signs* actually a dangerous dilution of the faith once and for all given to the saints? Or is it a hard-won, bedrock beginning point for those who find that their world has collapsed around them?

It is worth recalling once again the perspective of the writer of Ecclesiastes, for in this Old Testament book, the writer also portrays life as not always working out, even for those who are faithful. The eternal verities of Proverbs may be a good rule of thumb, for virtue is often rewarded. But not always. Its maxims must be taken as general affirmations, not hard-and-fast truth, for sometimes the good die young. Sometimes blessings rain on the unjust and evil on the just. Amorality, mystery, and death often prevail. What can we say given such hard reality? Certainly not much! As Qoheleth advises, God *"is in heaven and you are on earth, so don't say any more than you have to" (5:2)*. The fact that *Signs* risks any affirmations is as surprising as Qoheleth's own occasional recognition that God calls us to enjoy life's gifts when we are enabled to do so.

Tellingly, Qoheleth shuns the use of personal references or names for God. He neither says "my" God nor calls that God by his revealed name, Yahweh. In the Book of Ecclesiastes, the only pronoun attached to the divine is in 12:1, where in an act of extreme faith, the writer encourages readers to remember "your Creator." The use of Yahweh, a name associated with God's rescue of his people from bondage in Israel and one that means literally "I am he who is (available for you)," is avoided. What can one say when God is so distant? Rather than use the name his religious community believed revelatory of God's very character, something life's circumstances have called into doubt, Qoheleth can speak only generically of Elohim, the name for God that applies across all religious traditions.

Graham's discovery that "God" (even a generic "God") is present even in the midst of his hell on earth brings him hope. The fact that he can hold up the importance of such chiseled belief in a time of radical crisis (even if for a time the cross was but an indelible memory on the wall of his life) should cause believers to have hope, not suspicion. This is certainly its effect for Graham. For this grieving husband and father, it becomes simply a given that God is in charge. Everything that happens, even the evil, the suffering, that which is "random," must somehow be in his hand. Graham's painful yet liberating insight echoes that of Qoheleth: *"Everything that happens in this world happens at the time God chooses" (3:1). "Think about what God has done. . . . God sends both happiness and trouble; you never know what is going to happen next" (7:13–14)*. Though mystery remains concerning how such affirmations can square with God's gracious presence, how God and evil can be spoken of in the same breath without making God the cause of evil, Graham, like the writers of the Old Testament, chooses to root life's paradox here. *"God made everything, and you can no more understand what he does than you understand how new life begins in the womb of a pregnant woman" (11:5)*.

Both Shyamalan and Qoheleth would have us believe that despite surface appearances, this is God's domain. What they present to their audience is not an apologetic but a witness. Their narratives are not so much a solution to life's enigma as a reflection of a fundamental decision. As Jacques Ellul summarizes Qoheleth's thought, "To believe in God is to see [that] the facts of the world are not the end of the matter."[13] With this conviction, Shyamalan's characters are able to seize the day, at least that portion that God in his freedom and grace gives to them. *"Do your planting in the morning and in the evening, too. You never know whether it will all grow well or whether one planting will do better than the other" (11:6).* Graham comes to believe that life on the farm will continue for his family, despite all uncertainty. Given such faith in Elohim his Creator, he can again turn in belief to Yahweh his Redeemer. The faded outline of the cross on his bedroom wall again becomes for him a three-dimensional reality. He is able to put on his collar and embrace his vocation. God is, after all, *"the one Shepherd of us all" (12:11).*

8

CONFESSIONS
OF A WORKAHOLIC

Alexander Payne, *Election,*
and *About Schmidt*

> Dear Ndugu . . . What difference has my life made to anyone?
> None that I can think of. None at all. Hope things are fine with you.
> Yours truly, Warren Schmidt
>
> from the movie *About Schmidt*

Like Paul Thomas Anderson, Alexander Payne situates his movies in his hometown. *Citizen Ruth* (1996), *Election* (1999), and *About Schmidt* (2002) all take place in Omaha. "Nobody had done Omaha before," he said. "I thought it would be fun."[1] Payne, therefore, goes to great lengths to bring this Midwestern city to life, finding authentic locations, casting untrained townspeople and local actors in key roles, and re-creating authentic interior sets right down to the wallpaper. Though the novels that formed the basis of Payne's last two movies were set on the two coasts, Payne and his cowriter, Jim Taylor, simply relocated their screenplays to the Midwest. As a result, very different stories emerged.

People who live in Omaha vouch for the verisimilitude of the settings for Payne's movies.[2] Yet they also remain somewhat uneasy with what they see, for geography functions as more than a simple backdrop in Payne's movies. Omaha becomes, in fact, almost an additional character—*the* character. Payne's movies portray common concerns in everyday life—the debate over abortion, the politics of a high school election, the ennui of retirement. In doing so, however, they do not focus on the situations but on a "Midwestern" approach to them, an approach grounded in an old-fashioned work ethic, a stolid stoicism, and a social conservatism. Here is the source of discomfort for those who live in Omaha. Much like the writer of Ecclesiastes, Payne treats these "wholesome" values of his youth ironically, finding them wanting. Even those not from the Midwest wince, for such values, even if in exaggerated form, are too close to their own.

The words in Ecclesiastes derive much of their energy from their criticism of those "traditional" Israelites who absolutized the everyday wisdom of the Book of Proverbs, turning its sage observations into mandates that had to be followed. In a similar vein, Payne's stories score their punches by revealing the vanity of an undialectic commitment to Protestant Midwestern values. Life simply is not all motherhood and apple pie, hard work and traditional values, despite what some would have us believe. Just as in Qoheleth's day, a kind of denial is operative in much of society, thinks Payne, that invites exposure.[3] Everything is superficially judged fine, even when it is not. Answers are thought clear, even when they are not. This juxtaposition of the declared/imagined with the real fuels much of the humor in Payne's movies and provides their ironic bite. In the process, viewers are forced to confront the ambiguity of their own perceptions.

Payne's movies are black comedies that provide human insight, even as they both entertain and keep their audience off kilter. In each of them, viewers are confronted with a set of paradoxes, reality being other than what the characters perceive. For example, *Citizen Ruth* skewers both those who are pro-choice and those who are pro-life as it uses the abortion debate to criticize single-minded ideologues of whatever stripe. Ruth, a pregnant, pathetic huffer, who is once again putting her fetus at risk by her chemical sniffing, is given the choice by a judge between jail and abortion. As a result, advocates who are pro-choice and those who are pro-life jump to her defense, and she becomes a "celebrity." Ostensibly, she is the focus of these do-gooders' attention, but in actuality, she is not. As the movie ends, she walks away anonymously through the crowds while the two sides continue to fight bitterly over their real concern, the *laws* governing Ruth. The protestors are too consumed with the objective rightness, not to mention righteousness, of their positions to notice the real person in all her ambiguity and need.

In *Election*, through the voice-overs of the leading characters, viewers are given four competing points of view concerning the election of a student body president at George Washington Carver High School. These competing narrative perspectives not only challenge one another but also often contradict what these characters' actions on the screen would indicate. Reality is not always what we think or say. In *About Schmidt*, viewers are let in on some of Warren Schmidt's inner struggles following his retirement, despite his outward Midwestern stoicism, through a series of letters he writes to Ndugu, a young African boy whom he supports with monthly contributions. As with the characters in *Election,* Warren is not a wholly reliable narrator, either as to what is happening or to what he is feeling. The letters, read aloud by Schmidt, reveal three levels of "truth" simultaneously: what Warren has been conditioned to say and believe, what he is willing to risk questioning given his pain, and what viewers see portrayed on the screen.

Life does not always unfold as we might like or expect or even say. Our best efforts, our hardest work, sometimes do not produce anything worthwhile or meaningful. A contradiction often exists between what we project as reality and what turns out to be true, between what should be and what is, between the values we work for and the life that results. This gap—this void, this uncomfortable space between our projections and our reality—is the territory in which both Payne and the writer of Ecclesiastes reside. Here is the real setting, the one that lies beneath all their constructed settings. Here is what produces both the irony and the gloom that fill their skies, both literally and figuratively. Both of these sages force us to ask, Given life's messiness, does our work, our effort, really matter? *"Oh yes, I know what they say: 'If you obey God, everything will be all right, but it will not go well for the wicked. . . .' But this is nonsense. Look at what happens in the world"* (8:12–14).

Election

With a budget of $8.5 million, this MTV-made teenage comedy set in an American high school is an unlikely candidate for one of 1999's most memorable movies. But *Election* holds its own, even against such standouts as *Magnolia* and *American Beauty.* It garnered an Oscar nomination and a Writers Guild of America Award for best adapted screenplay, an Artios for best casting in a comedy, an Eddie nomination for best editing in a comedy, a Golden Globe nomination for best actress in a comedy, and an Independent Spirit Award for best director. Smartly written and carefully structured, this biting and sometimes subversive dark comedy deals ostensibly with the politics of a student council election. However, the story also satirizes all forms of politics. Looking at Tracy, one of Carver High School's candidates for student body president, we might think we are seeing a teenage Hilary Clinton or Elizabeth Dole, but we also see ourselves, for Payne's *polis* is as broad as life itself. In Jim McAllister, the civics instructor, and in Tracy, Paul, and Tammy, the three candidates, we see our struggles and ourselves. We too ask the question, How can our efforts prove meaningful given life's randomness and mystery?

Election deals with the gap between the "Midwestern" (American? Protestant?) belief that hard work should and will bring both success and happiness and the realities of life, which often contradict this belief. As the writer of Ecclesiastes rhetorically asks, *"You spend your life working, laboring, and what do you have to show for it?" (1:3).* Our commitment to success all too often proves hollow: *"Then I thought about all that I had done and how hard I had worked doing it, and I realized that it didn't mean a thing" (2:11).* Rather than issuing forth in happiness, our toil results in an all too common experience of loneliness. *"How can you keep warm by yourself?"* *(4:11)*. Life, it seems, does not support our efforts to be *"too good or too wise" (7:16)*. Destiny doesn't always work out to our advantage. Life remains ultimately unknowable. *"Look at what happens in the world: sometimes the righteous get the punishment of the wicked, and the wicked get the reward of the righteous. I say it is useless" (8:14)*.

The plot of *Election* is a simple one. George Washington Carver High School (ironically, an almost all white school) is having its student body elections. Much to the chagrin of Jim McAllister (Matthew Broderick), the popular social science teacher and adviser to the student council, the only candidate running is Tracy Flick (Reese Witherspoon), an overachieving sweet-talker who is a Goody Two-Shoes. Not wanting her to win, both because she is too smug and because his best friend and colleague lost his job and his family after having an affair with her, McAllister secretly persuades the likeable but not too bright quarterback on the football team, Paul Metzler (Chris Klein), to run. When his sister, Tammy (Jessica Campbell), also announces she is in the race (to get back at a former girlfriend who has jilted her for her brother), the movie's setup (and the election slate) is complete.

What sets this movie apart from other teen comedies is not just Payne's ability to capture the feel of high school life, in particular, student council elections. Rather, it is his ability to make us as viewers care who wins. We come to know each of the four main characters and end up being concerned about what happens to them, even the obnoxious Tracy. Though each is typecast (the popular teacher who literally lives at the school, the overachieving student who hides her ambition behind a veneer of affable perkiness, the football jock who is sincere but not too bright, and the campus rebel [in this case a sophomore girl who is experimenting with her sexual orientation]), none remains a caricature. We can see ourselves and our friends in them, even as they are lampooned.

Through the not always reliable narration of his lead characters, Payne provides us with four spins on what is happening, four points of view. Here is the locus of the movie's power and the source of its meaning. We not only see what the characters are doing, but we also hear them describe both themselves and their rivals. Jim McAllister, for example, talks about being closer than ever to his wife, Diane, after nine years of marriage, even as we watch him sneak down to the basement late at night to watch pornographic videos. McAllister also first introduces us to Tracy, whose narration even includes several freeze-frames of her face contorted with a smirk (the way he wants to picture her). McAllister explains why he dislikes Tracy by telling of her affair with his colleague, even while viewers see how Mr. Novotny used his position of authority as a teacher to manipulate the insecure Tracy. McAllister is now convinced that Tracy must learn life's important lesson that you can't always win, and he feels destined in that enterprise to be her teacher! But even as he is speaking, the audience senses this teacher's ambivalence toward his pupil—there is both fear and fascination. *"The wise may claim to know, but they don't" (8:17).* Life is not easily parsed.

Jim McAllister is the school's most popular teacher, having won the best teacher award three times. But though he has achieved much, there is also a numbing monotony to his life. He goes to school early each morning, gives the same lectures over and over, then goes home to a relationship that has become merely routine. Tracy puts it this way: "Now that I have more life experience, I feel sorry for Mr. McAllister. I mean, anyone who's stuck in the same little room, wearing the same stupid clothes, saying the same exact things year after year, for his whole life, while his students go to good colleges and move to big cities and to great things and make loads of money, he's got to be at least a little jealous." Or as the writer of Ecclesiastes concludes, *"Life is useless, all useless. You spend your life working, laboring, and what do you have to show for it? . . . Everything leads to weariness—a weariness too great for words. . . . What has been done before will be done again. There is nothing new in the whole world" (1:2–3, 8–9).*

McAllister has reached a dead end in his life and is feeling middle aged ahead of schedule. Pressured in both his personal and his professional lives, he is no longer able to see things clearly. (Payne gives viewers a pathetically humorous visual clue as to McAllister's state when a bee stings him on the eyelid and the swelling causes him to become one-eyed.) When his friendship with Dave Novotny's ex-wife, Linda, crosses the line as a hug leads to hormonal pas-

Jim McAllister (Matthew Broderick), a social science teacher and adviser to the student council, with Tracy Flick (Reese Witherspoon), who is running for student body president. *Election* (d. Payne, 1999). Photo by Bob Akester. © 1999 Paramount Pictures. All rights reserved.

sion, McAllister rationalizes, "There was no turning back. It was a miracle. What had blossomed between Linda and me was too real, too powerful to deny." Payne drives home the unreality of McAllister's judgment by showing him driving a sports car on the coast of Italy, only for the image to morph into the Ford Fiesta he is actually driving. His Italian designer shoes become what they in fact are, unstylish Hush Puppies.

Similarly, when the student counters for the election inform McAllister, their adviser, that Tracy has won by one vote, the camera zooms in for a close-up of the one-eyed teacher. Seeing Tracy through this skewed perspective jumping up and down with glee outside the classroom where the votes are being tallied, McAllister reasons, "I had to stop her now." If he can save Carver from Tracy, he will have finally made a difference. And so two ballots are slipped into the trash can, the votes are tallied once again, Paul Metzler is declared the winner, and no one seems the wiser.

But destiny has other plans. Linda tells Jim's wife of his indiscretion with her and his subsequent desire for a tryst, while the janitor finds the two discarded votes when he is emptying the trash.

Predictably, McAllister loses everything and ends up as a guide at the Museum of Natural History in New York City after a lengthy job search. Although we laugh at McAllister's ludicrous life, his pain is also real, and we as viewers feel it viscerally. We wince, for example, when we watch him explaining the democratic process to Paul Metzler by drawing "indistinguishable" circles on the chalkboard and saying that just as we need both apples and oranges, the democratic process needs two candidates. This turns into laughter when Paul densely responds, "I also like bananas." How often have we voted for indistinguishable circles? We groan as we watch McAllister pathetically groping Linda as the camera films the scene from her baby's point of view. McAllister's pain is achingly real, too close at times to our own. *My life has been useless, but in it I have seen everything. Some good people may die while others live on, even though they are evil. So don't be too good or too wise—why kill yourself? But don't be too wicked or too foolish, either—why die before you have to? Avoid both extremes" (7:15–18).*

Tracy Flick, McAllister's antagonist, is a person who lives on by shear effort, someone who manages to go far in life though she is unlikable. An overzealous overachiever, she follows in the steps of her single mom, who has improved herself by becoming a paralegal secretary and who writes to successful women such as Elizabeth Dole, asking them to give her daughter tips as to how they did it. It would seem that Tracy's single-focused ambition comes naturally and is, thus, at least partially understandable. She sees herself as the rags-to-riches Horatio Alger, the poor kid who will succeed by hard work and effort. It is, after all, the American way. When the rich kid, Paul Metzler, decides to run against Tracy, she just sets her jaw more firmly, leans on her campaign button-making machine more strongly, and says in a voice-over, "I had to work a little harder, that's all." Like McAllister, she too appeals to the democratic ideal, believing that voters know that this country was built "by people just like me who work very hard and don't have everything handed to them on a silver spoon." As we see her boarding the school bus and Paul getting into the new pickup truck his parents have given him, Tracy's voice rises as she criticizes Paul for thinking he can "waltz right in and with no qualifications whatsoever . . . try to take away what other people have worked for very, very hard their entire lives! No! It didn't bother me at all." Viewers know better.

At the election assembly in the gymnasium, where all three candidates give their speeches, Paul mumbles something about how he is used to winning on the football field and "we can all score a winning touchdown together." Though the students intially jeer Tammy, his younger sister, she wins them over with her extemporaneous speech: "Who cares about this stupid election? We all know it doesn't matter. . . . You really think it's going to change anything around here, make one single person smarter or happier or nicer? . . . The same pathetic charade happens every year." Tracy, on the other hand, intones sincerely, "I care about Carver, and I care about each and every one of you, and together we can all make a difference." It is painful to listen. Do any of them have a clue?

On the eve of the election, we see each of the three candidates praying in their respective rooms:

> Tracy: Dear Lord Jesus, I do not often speak with you and ask for things, but now I really must insist that you help me win the election tomorrow. . . . Put me in office where I belong so that I may carry out your will on earth as it is in heaven.

> Tammy: Dear God, I know I don't believe in you, but since I'll be starting Catholic school soon, I thought I should at least practice. . . . Let's see, what do I want?

> Paul: Dear God, thank you for all your blessings . . . good health, nice parents, a nice truck, and what I'm told is a large penis, and I'm very grateful.

Tracy might seem the least objectionable choice for president, despite her pushiness, but she has secrets in her closet as well, and ambition has blinded her too. Mr. Novotny had been able to seduce her by telling her, "Sometimes people like you have to pay a price for their greatness. And that price is loneliness." As we watch him kiss Tracy and drive her to his house, where he seduces this "girl" not with champagne but with root beer, we hear Tracy confidently assert, "It was the first time somebody ever saw the real me, that me that nobody else knows." Tracy will do anything for greatness. When she accidentally falls to the ground while trying to retape her campaign sign to the brick wall, ripping down her banner in the process, she responds by tearing down all the signs of the others as well. With red-stained hands reminiscent of Lady MacBeth, Tracy takes the wadded up banners to a dumpster and discards them.

Just as with McAllister, Payne has fun with his portrayals of Tracy, but again, Payne skates successfully on the edge, not losing the audience's uncomfortable identification with her. When, for example, McAllister asks Tracy early in the campaign when she is still running unopposed why she is bothering to put up posters, she responds, "Coca-Cola is the number one soft drink company in the world without any major competitors. But they spend millions of dollars on advertising. I guess that's how come they stay number one." This comparison of Tracy to Coke is brought back ironically in the epilogue when McAllister, years later, is attending a museum conference in Washington, D.C., and happens to see Tracy leave a government building and climb into a limousine. McAllister has just finished saying that he now feels sorry for Tracy: "I mean, when I think about my new life and all the exciting things I'm doing and I think about what her life must be like, probably still getting up at five in the morning to pursue her pathetic little dreams, it just makes me sad. I mean, where is she really trying to get to anyway?" But then he sees Tracy get into the limo, and his old resentments surface. "Who the f— does she think she is?" McAllister yells as he heaves a cup of the Pepsi he has been drinking at the limo. *I have also learned why people work so hard to succeed: it is because they envy the things their neighbors have. But it is useless. It is like chasing the wind. They say that we would be fools to fold our hands and let ourselves starve to death. Maybe so, but it is better to have only a little, with peace of mind, than be busy all the time with both hands, trying to catch the wind"* (4:4–6).

The only character who rises above the fray is Paul Metzler, the dense but popular football player. Though he is naive, he is also sincere in his relations with others. When he prays on the night before the election, he also prays for his sister's well-being. When he goes to school on election day to vote, he wishes Tracy good luck and then unknowingly casts the deciding vote for her because he's not sure "it's right to vote for yourself." After being declared the new president, Paul enters a coffee shop with his parents where McAllister is eating. Excited by his victory, Paul asks his teacher if it would be a good thing to plan a carnival for muscular dystrophy. Even after having his presidency rescinded, Paul, we are told in the epilogue, had a good senior year, got into Nebraska, and threw a big party. He seems to live out Qoheleth's advice: *"Young people, enjoy your youth. Be happy while you are still young. Do what you want to do, and follow your heart's desire. . . . Don't let anything worry you or cause you pain. You aren't going to be young very long" (11:9–10).*

About Schmidt

In *Election,* Alexander Payne lampooned those who thought they could figure out life. Whether seeking to parse the difference between ethics and morality or letting one's work take over one's life, whether rationalizing one's feelings of loneliness as the price of greatness or foolishly committing one's self to success at all costs, Payne's characters seek in vain to manage life, to control their destinies. But as Tracy herself declared at the beginning of the movie, "You can't interfere with destiny. That's why it's destiny." If you try, "you'll just suffer." Viewers end up asking the question neither Tracy nor McAllister will ask: *"What do we gain from all our work?" (3:9).*

In *About Schmidt,* Payne returns to this same theme, though from the perspective not of a high schooler beginning a career but of a person facing retirement. What have all his efforts amounted to? Even at the movie's end, as Warren Schmidt (Jack Nicholson) returns from his daughter's wedding in Denver, he reads in a voice-over a letter he has just written to Ndugu, his six-year-old African friend and confidant. Having seen at a roadstop an exhibit on the early pioneers who crossed Nebraska heading West, Schmidt expresses his frustration at not having been able to do anything that might make his life significant:

My trip to Denver is so insignificant compared to the journeys others have taken. . . . I know we're all pretty small in the big scheme of things, and I suppose the most you can hope for is to make some kind of difference. But what kind of difference have I made? What in the world is better because of me? When I was out in Denver, I tried to do the right thing, tried to convince Jeannie she was making a big mistake, but I failed. Now she's married to that nincompoop and there's nothing I can do about it. I am weak, and I am a failure. There's just no getting around it. Relatively soon I will die. . . . Once I am dead and everyone who knew me dies too, it will be as though I never even existed. What difference has my life made to anyone? None that I can think of. None at all. Hope things are fine with you.

Yours truly, Warren Schmidt

It is true: *"In spite of all our work there is nothing we can take with us. It isn't right! We go just as we came. We labor, trying to catch the wind, and what do we get? We get to live our lives in darkness and grief, worried, angry, and sick"* (5:15–17).

As *About Schmidt* opens, the camera gives us a visual tour of Omaha. It is gray and overcast. Always in the picture is the Woodmen of the World tower.[4] As the camera draws closer to it, the reason becomes clear. We see Warren Schmidt sitting in his office on one of the upper floors in the building, with packing boxes containing all his files stacked neatly along one of the walls. The camera looks down on him from above as Warren, expressionless in a room stripped clean, sits watching the second hand of the clock tick toward five o'clock. It is Warren's last day on the job as assistant vice president and actuariate at Woodmen of the World Insurance Company. His job has been to predict the deaths of its clients for this insurance company. As the second hand reaches the twelve, Warren turns off the lights and exits into a rainy night as the title of the movie appears. Given his predictable death, how then is Warren Schmidt to live? *"Oh, I know, 'Wisdom is better than foolishness, just as light is better than darkness. The wise can see where they are going, and fools cannot.' But I also know that the same fate is waiting for us all. I thought to myself, 'What happens to fools is*

going to happen to me, too. So what have I gained from being so wise?'
'Nothing,' I answered, 'not a thing'" (2:13–15).

The scene switches to Warren and his wife, Helen (June Squibb), driving to Johnny's Café, a steak house where Warren's retirement dinner is being held. As we enter we are shown a series of pictures of prize-winning Omaha steers, then the retirement picture of Warren, followed by the bas-relief of an Indian chief on the restaurant wall in the distance. This metaphor of cows/humans being led to the slaughter recurs throughout the movie. During the scene of Helen's funeral, for example, a cattle trailer is being hosed off. The cows have been delivered to the slaughterhouse. Cattle trucks pass Warren while he is driving, and a side of beef is served at his daughter's wedding reception. *"After all, the same fate awaits human beings and animals alike. One dies just like the other. They are the same kind of creature. A human being is no better off than an animal, because life has no meaning for either. They are both going to the same place—the dust"* (3:19–20). Warren's young replacement tells him during his remarks at the retirement dinner to stop by and visit him in his old office. He might have some questions, and there will be new products. But when Warren later does this, he is ignored, and his boxes of files are on the loading dock, going to either storage or the dumpster. *"You work for something with all your wisdom, knowledge, and skill, and then you have to leave it all to someone who hasn't had to work for it. It is useless, and it isn't right!"* (2:21). What has been Warren's primary source of meaning in his life is gone. He is, it would seem, but a steer on the way to the slaughterhouse.

At the dinner, Warren's old friend, Ray Nichols (Len Cariou), stands up to toast Warren and give him some perspective on his retirement. The gifts and the dinner don't mean a thing, he tells Warren. What is meaningful is that he devoted his life to being productive while working for a fine company, raising a fine family, building a fine home, being respected in his community, and having lasting friendships. Ray offers a paean of praise to those solid Midwestern values, centered in the Protestant work ethic, that Americans cherish, despite their misgivings that life will indeed work out. Ray concludes, "At the end of his career, if a man can look back and say, 'I did it, I did my job,' then he can retire in glory and enjoy riches far beyond the monetary kind. So all of you young people here," Ray intones, "take a very good look at a very rich man."

Here is the setup. Here is how we have been taught that it should be! The problem is, Warren knows it is a lie. He is poor in spirit. The platitudes are more than he can endure. Telling Helen that he will be right back, Schmidt goes to the bar in the next room for a vodka gimlet. But even Warren can't bring himself to fully question the truth. He explains to his daughter, Jeannie (Hope Davis), who calls him later that evening, that the party went just fine. "Nice event." And then continuing the lie, he thanks her and Randall (Dermot Mulroney), her boyfriend, for the robe they gave him.

How is life to have meaning when work is taken from you? Warren has no clue as he goes through the first days of his retirement doing the Scrambled Word Game and watching TV in his tie and sweater. While channel surfing, he hears about Childreach, a sponsor-a-child agency that seeks to bring hope to African orphans. Sponsors have to give just $22 per month. Warren signs up. When the confirmation of his child arrives in the mail and he

Warren Schmidt (Jack Nicholson) at his retirement dinner. *About Schmidt* (d. Payne, 2003). © 2003 New Line Cinema. All rights reserved.

is asked to write a note to his orphan, Warren begins to reveal to this six-year-old boy, Ndugu, what he has not allowed himself to admit aloud to anyone.*

Schmidt wonders, for example, "Who is this old woman who lives in my house? Why is it that every little thing she does irritates me?" The camera zooms in on Helen as Warren is narrating his thoughts to Ndugu, focusing on her armpit and unattractive wrinkles. But to make his life even more problematic, when Warren returns home from mailing the letter to Ndugu and getting a Blizzard at Dairy Queen, he finds his wife dead on the kitchen floor from a blood clot in her brain. Soon, filled with remorse for his judgmental thoughts and feeling alone, he begins to miss her. Again, events for Warren go from bad to worse, however, as he discovers in Helen's closet old love letters from his close friend Ray. Incensed over this long-ago affair, Warren throws out all of Helen's clothes and angrily confronts his friend.

Work, spouse . . . children! Warren and Helen had one child, Jeannie, who now lives in Denver. She is engaged to be married to a waterbed salesman by the name of Randall, who at Helen's funeral tries to sell Warren on a pyramid scheme. Warren tries to talk her out of marrying Randall, not by confronting her directly, something his Midwestern reticence makes difficult, but by implying that Helen didn't approve of Randall. Schmidt also asks Jeannie to stay for several weeks longer ("Who's gonna take care of me?"), but to no one's surprise, she refuses. Estranged from his daughter and angry that she is marrying beneath her (and himself!), Warren is left alone at the airport as the two of them fly home.

The movie's setup is complete. Today will be the first day of the rest of his life, a time period that Warren Schmidt, as an actuary, has actually figured out. In his second letter to Ndugu, he confesses, "It's just me and my thoughts, knocking around this big old house." Explaining to this uncomprehending six-year-old

---

*Ndugu is Alexander Payne's creation and does not appear in the novel by Louis Begley that Payne and his cowriter, Jim Taylor, adapted. This proves a wonderful conceit, allowing viewers to understand something of the complexity of Schmidt through this unreliable narrator.

what his job had been, Schmidt says he "can calculate with great probability how long [a] man will live. In my own case, now that my wife has died, there is a 73 percent chance I will die within nine years provided that I do not remarry. . . . Life is short, Ndugu, and I can't afford to waste another minute." *"A wise person thinks about death" (7:4).*

After years of both a predictable work schedule and someone to watch over him, Warren barely knows how to take care of himself. In another letter to Ndugu, Warren tries to put his best face forward: "This house is under new management. You'd never know the difference." Viewers see differently, however. The cupboards are bare, dishes and trash are everywhere, frozen dinners have become his staple, and his car has broken down. Warren looks a wreck. One night while sleeping fitfully, Schmidt decides he will drive to Denver and talk Jeannie out of her marriage. Getting into his new Winnebago Adventurer, something Helen had gotten them for their retirement years, Warren sets off on a road trip "with" Ndugu as his traveling buddy. Viewers are thus ushered into what will prove to be a traditional road movie, one in which the events along the way are less important than the insight achieved.

To no one's surprise, Jeannie doesn't want her father to come to Denver until a few days before the wedding. So Warren decides he will make his time meaningful by paying a visit to important places in his past. He tells Ndugu that he wants to clear a few cobwebs from his memory, given that "so much has happened in my life." Again, however, Schmidt's efforts to fix life's meaning fail. He drives to Holdrege, Nebraska, where he was born, but the site of his birth sixty-six years earlier is now a tire store. Rationalizing his disappointment to Ndugu, he says it was nevertheless good to be home again. Next, he visits his old fraternity at the University of Kansas but finds the current members unimpressed by his presence. Again, he hides his pain, ludicrously telling Ndugu, "I highly recommend you pledge a fraternity when you go to college." Schmidt drives on, stopping to visit the Custer County Museum to see its arrowhead collection. Nearby, he learns from a Native American convenience store worker that the Indians "got a raw deal." He is shocked! Warren's past provides little solace or significance.

Work, spouse, family, heritage—none of them seems to hold any promise of providing meaning for Warren's life. Rather, the first ray of insight, however painfully it is gained, dawns when he drives his thirty-five-foot Winnebago into an RV park and is invited to dinner by a stranger who admires his oversized vehicle. After sitting in the living room of the Rusks (who own a Famous Footwear franchise in Wisconsin) and looking at their snapshots, Warren finds himself alone with Vicki when her husband goes to the store for more beer. Vicki chooses to be honest with Warren, telling him that though he has put on a pretty good face, "I think inside you're a sad man. . . . I see something more than grief and loss in you. Something deeper. . . . My guess, it's anger . . . fear, loneliness." Mistaking her care for him with attraction to him, Warren tells Vicki that she understands him better than his wife, Helen, did even after forty-two years. When she responds, "Oh, you sad man," he shockingly leans over and kisses her on the mouth. Violated, the woman kicks him out, screaming. Warren is honestly perplexed. He has rarely if ever had anyone befriend him, particularly a woman, and he simply doesn't have a clue as to the dynamics. All he can do is apologize, jump into his Adventurer, and flee into the night.

Honesty has its effect, however. Soon Warren stops to call Ray to tell him he is reconsidering his anger in light of their years of friendship (even though he accidentally erases the message and then chooses not to leave another). Later, Warren pulls off the road and stops for the night beside the Missouri River. As he sits on the top of his RV and looks up at the stars, he finds himself asking Helen, "What did you really think of me?" "Were you disappointed but too nice to show it?" "I forgive you for Ray." "I let you down. I'm sorry, Helen. Will you forgive me?" As a shooting star streaks across the sky, Warren makes the sign of the cross without thinking. His confession has been a holy moment, though not also without its humor.

Roger Ebert, therefore, exaggerates when he suggests that *About Schmidt* "is not about a man who goes on a journey to find himself, because there is no one to find,"[5] for the audience has witnessed Warren getting in touch with himself for the first time in years. Old patterns die hard, however. Awaking from his night along the river, Warren commits himself anew to blocking his daughter's wedding. This will be his life's purpose. In the minutes that follow, we are introduced to Jeannie's future in-laws through Warren's eyes. Randall's mother, Roberta (Kathy Bates), is a lusty, post-hippie who is both figuratively and literally larger than life. She swears at her ex-husband, drinks Manhattans in the afternoon, brags that her son is "something special" because she breast-fed him until he was almost five, speaks openly about her hysterectomy, eats chicken sloppily with her fingers, talks about how Jeannie and her Randall have a "white hot" sex life, and tries to seduce Warren while naked in the hot tub. When Warren wakes up too stiff to move after a night on Randall's waterbed, Roberta nurses him with chicken soup, even asking if he has used his bedpan. Warren is still a kid it seems, someone needing to be cared for, and Roberta is there to help.

Not surprisingly, Warren's efforts to stop the wedding fail miserably. Jeannie fires back, "All of a sudden you're taking an interest in what I do. You have an opinion about my life now!" She instructs her father in no uncertain terms, "You are going to come to my wedding, and you are going to sit there and enjoy it." And he does. Warren even gives a toast to the new couple at the reception. After a long pause, he first mentions how pleased Helen was that Jeannie had found a companion, a partner. He continues, stammering, "What I really want to say . . . what I want to say, what I really want to say is . . . thank you, to you Randall, for taking such good care of my daughter . . . on this special day, this very special day, that I am very . . . pleased." Jeannie sits motionless, perhaps breathing a sigh of relief and even giving a faint smile.

Some movie critics believe that at the wedding, Warren in this way has failed himself, has reverted to those earlier Midwestern insincerities and platitudes. After all, Warren even seems to admit as much as he tells Ndugu in a letter that he tried to do the right thing, that he tried to convince Jeannie not to marry Randall, but that he was weak and a failure. At a deeper level, however, at the level of "being" and not of "doing," Warren has succeeded. He has evidenced for the second time since he set off on his journey of discovery a newly found sensitivity. He has chosen an act of unconditional love. He has chosen to support his daughter, stand with her, even if she is making a mistake. He has realized that Roberta and Randall love her and will support her. Here is something to affirm.

The road trip over, the movie winds to an end, but not without a final surprising event. Returning home, Warren sorts through his mail and finds a letter from Ndugu. It is written for him by Sister Nadine, who cares for Ndugu in the orphanage. She explains, "Ndugu and I want you to know that he receives all of your letters. He hopes that you are happy in your life and healthy. He thinks of you every day, and he wants very much your happiness. Ndugu is only six years old and cannot read or write, but he has made for you a painting. He hopes that you will like his painting." Warren unfolds the sheet of paper and looks at a simple watercolor of two stick figures holding hands under a blue sky and a bright sun. Warren Schmidt begins to cry, despite his stoic demeanor, and then through the tears to smile.

The gift of friendship, which the picture represents, is not first of all about the $22 per month that Warren gives. It is that, but it is also more. Ndugu has accepted Warren's friendship from afar and has tried to reciprocate in the only way he knows how. Henry David Thoreau once said, "Most men lead lives of quiet desperation."[6] And they go to the grave with the song still in them. Warren has been able to get his melody out. Whether Ray understands, or Jeannie, at least Ndugu does. Though life's loneliness and banality prevail, Warren has been able to seize the day, to love another. While his job at Woodmen had taught him how to manage death, it had not prepared him for how to live. This was a more difficult lesson, yet one a small boy could teach him. A story that might have been simply a black comedy has become a journey of self-realization. Schmidt does not have to do anything; it is enough simply to be who he is. There might not be a tidy resolution, but there is a relationship. *"So I realized that all we can do is be happy and do the best we can while we are still alive. All of us should eat and drink and enjoy what we have worked for. It is God's gift"* (3:12–13).

Those seeing Jack Nicholson on this unconventional road trip cannot help but recall his breakout role as the pothead lawyer in *Easy Rider* (1969). Warren Schmidt is another of Nicholson's antiheroes, though this time possessing a sad sweetness. No longer the young rebel embarking on a career, Nicholson is now an unimaginative, stout middle American with a comb-over, someone who has lost his way in life. He is "everyman," just an ordinary guy gone sour. Viewers have met Warren Schmidt before—as Homer Simpson and Ralph Kramden, Willy Loman and Rabbit Angstrom.[7] There are similarities to that quintessential Midwestern ordinary man, George Babbitt, the Ohio real estate salesman. But where Babbitt remains to this day the embodiment of narrow-mindedness and self-satisfaction, someone unable to escape his cautious confines, Schmidt is able to break free from his Midwestern chains. While Babbitt tells his son, Ted, at the novel's end, "I've never done a single thing I've wanted to in my whole life," Schmidt learns initial lessons in forgiveness and tolerance as he and Ndugu complete their road trip together. Confusion turns to insight. Love that has grown stale starts to blossom. Death that has been dreaded becomes the window to life. This love is fragile to be sure, the insight slight. Death will still overtake. But life also proves precious. *"Sorrow is better than laughter; it may sadden your face, but it sharpens your understanding. Someone who is always thinking about happiness is a fool. A wise person thinks about death" (7:3–4).*

Confessions of a Workaholic

My first article as a young professor was titled "'Confessions of a Workaholic': A Reappraisal of Qoheleth."[8] In it I argued that the very best of contemporary Old Testament scholarship—that of Walter Brueggemann and Gerhard von Rad—had trouble maintaining a consistent stance toward Old Testament wisdom.[9] While at times recognizing that Israel's wisdom literature called humankind to enjoy life as a gift from God, to "be" and not just to "do," these teachers (and other modern biblical scholars) more typically described Israel's wisdom as an attempt to describe how we might order life.

Brueggemann, for example, in his wonderful article "Scripture and an Ecumenical Life-Style," discussed the fivefold nature of biblical wisdom. His fourth thesis was that the biblical sages recognized "that life has been called good (Gen. 1:31), that it is for our enjoyment, celebration, appreciation."[10] But in reworking this article for his opening chapter in his book *In Man We Trust*, Brueggemann changed this assertion about wisdom to read, "Man is meant for an orderly role in an orderly cosmos. His rightful destiny is to discern that order and find his responsible share of it."[11] What a difference! Are we to "celebrate life" or "find our responsible share in it"? That is, are we to seek to master life or at least manage it, or are we to appreciate it, learning how best to enjoy it?

Gerhard von Rad similarly defined wisdom's goal as being "to wrest from the chaos of events some kind of order in which man was not continually at the mercy of the incalculable." Yet at other times von Rad understood wisdom as being based in "the faculty of hearing."[12] Was wisdom, at its core, an ethical activity or an aesthetic one? There is an ambiguity in von Rad's thought. If the goal of Old Testament wisdom was and is to wrest some form of order from chaos, then Qoheleth's advice to enjoy while we can the "small" gifts that come our way from a distant God is meager advice indeed. It is cynical and pessimistic. His words are simply resigned and ironic conclusions that carry little motivation or consolation. On the other hand, if Ecclesiastes' advice to enjoy our work and play as we are able because they are a divine gift is a central tenant of the wisdom tradition, then Qoheleth's advice is not a sop but a challenge to those who see life's meaning as being dependent on their accomplishment. His words would not then be cynical but celebrative. Qoheleth's irony would open up readers not to a fatalism but to a recognition of common grace.

Here Alexander Payne can be of help, providing interpreters a helpful pair of eyeglasses. Though a few interpreters of his movies have been unable to get beyond his biting irony, seeing his films as portraying the denial of values *(Citizen Ruth)* and the meaninglessness of work *(Election* and *About Schmidt),* most have rightly seen that even his dark humor has a redemptive trajectory.

While the workweek of the average American shrunk for over one hundred years, the trend reversed itself in the last twenty-five years. We now work on average six more hours a week than we did in the late 1970s. Leisure time is also again on the decline, having shrunk on average more than a third during the mid-1980s and 1990s.

Couples work on average more than a month more each year than they did just a decade ago. Yet the majority of us know that this is not right. Sixty-four percent of us wish for a simpler life.[13]

Like Qoheleth, Payne exposes the futility of our efforts to wrest order from chaos, to produce meaning by our own efforts. He does this not to plunge us into a greater darkness but to help us turn from our futile efforts at self-definition. Payne holds up to the light of folly all attempts to discern life's order and to locate our responsible share of it. Better to be a dim-witted yet happy Paul Metzler than a Tracy Flick, to enjoy life as it unfolds than to watch life whither after we have tried to pick its blossoms.

But could there be another option? Warren Schmidt discovers that it is at the heart of our humanity to ask for forgiveness, to be tolerant, to accept the love of another. Warren Schmidt has done little, either at work or at home, that has had significance. Yet his tears as he comprehends Ndugu's drawing tell it all. *"Two are better off than one" (4:9)*. Though our work is vain, our life can be filled with meaning nonetheless.

9

HUMANITY
AT FULL STRETCH

Let the "Preacher" Respond

A classic cartoon shows an editor looking over a manuscript and saying, "Mr. Dickens, either it was the best of times or it was the worst of times. It can't be both."[1] But the fact of the matter is, it can! Sometimes life's extremities are experienced concurrently. Even in the midst of life's hellish particulars (we might even say, particularly amid life's hellish particulars), a useless beauty resides that bubbles to the surface and invites our attentive gaze. The preceding pages noted life's contradictions in both movie and biblical text—joy amid the dust. While focusing on the *grittiness* of everyday life, we have also been invited to gaze paradoxically at the *gift* of everyday life—at the plastic bag floating in the wind or the plastic spoon offering a taste of chocolate ice cream. Even given life's "evil and madness," we are to *"eat [our] food and be happy; drink [our] wine and be cheerful. It's all right with God" (9:3, 7)*. As we have listened to a dialogue between a group of movies and the Book of Ecclesiastes, we have encountered "humanity at full stretch."[2]

Both text and image offer what Don Saliers refers to as "the poetics of everyday life," in which our "imaginative powers lead us beyond the tyranny of the 'literally given.'" In a provocative address titled "Where Beauty and Terror Lie: The Poetics of Everyday Life," Saliers argues that the deepest things we can know are found not in abstract thought but in our embeddedness in life, in our defining affections and passions. He writes:

> A person or a society is better known through what is feared, loved, grieved over, and hoped for than through its factually stated ideas and thoughts. . . . A sense of transcendence in and through the finitude of the world will appear, if at all, precisely amid the contrasts and connections between terror and beauty.

Saliers recognizes that it can be dangerous to appeal to everyday, bodily life for meaning and significance. We are so inattentive at times, so egocentric and delusional. Our reason is also clouded. Nonetheless, "it is only in the stretch of seeing the world in its fullness, in critical awareness of our situatedness between the terrifying and the glorious, between the unspeakable and the most desirable, that we come to moral and religious maturity."[3]

Saliers's focus is the importance of religious ritual. The commingled laughter and tears at a funeral meal are paradigmatic for him. But Saliers's observation might equally apply to other forms of poetics. The terror and beauty resident in a subsection of contemporary movies provide viewers a similar window into life's meaning. They, too, provide the commingling of senseless loss and fragile delight. In the terror of life portrayed, we are provided glimpses of something more—fugitive energies that invite our gaze.

Not all of us want to look within such messiness. Some in the Christian community, for example, are eager to jump quickly ahead, to look to the end of the story—to the empty tomb and life in Christ. We want doxology without lament. We have, for this reason, tended to avoid these troubling movies while thinking that Ecclesiastes is a dangerous book. But we would do well to be reminded of Dietrich Bonhoeffer's prophetic words as he sat in a Nazi prison camp during Advent in 1943, awaiting a verdict that would ultimately mean his death:

> My thoughts and feelings seem to be getting more and more like those of the Old Testament, and in recent months I have been reading the Old Testament much more than the New. It is only when one knows the unutterability of the name of God that one can utter the name of Jesus Christ; it is only when one loves life and the earth so much that without them everything seems to be over that one may believe in the resurrection and a new world. . . . In my opinion it is not Christian to want to take our thoughts and feelings too quickly and too directly from the New Testament.

One day every tear will be wiped away—"Death will be no more; mourning and crying and pain will be no more, for the first things have passed away" (Rev. 21:4 NRSV). But we do not yet live in those days. We dare not, thought Bonhoeffer, "speak the last word before the last but one."[4]

Later, in a Christmas letter to his parents, Bonhoeffer noted that there was no special problem associated with being in a prison cell at Christmas, for "misery, suffering, poverty, loneliness, helplessness, and guilt" mean something different to God than they do to us: "Christ was born in a stable because there was no room for him in the inn." Prisoners understand this better than most others, Bonhoeffer suggested. This really is "glad tidings."[5] God is with us in the here and now. According to Bonhoeffer, we wrongly ignore the penultimate in life for the ultimate. We turn to the fullness of God's saving revelation in Jesus Christ, forsaking the frightening terror and fragile beauty resident in God's creatures and creation. There is more to the Story! There is also the terror and the beauty of the here and now, and it is in them that we as human beings come to maturity. For Bonhoeffer, everything has its time. It is presumptuous to desire everything at once. He noted, " 'For everything there is a season' (Eccles. 3:1); everything has its time: 'a time to weep and a time to laugh; . . . a time to embrace, and a time to refrain from embracing.' "[6]

Let the "Preacher" Respond

This book has put Ecclesiastes into conversation with recent movies not only to help clarify the deeper intentions of these films but also to bring the biblical text to life once again. Readers of Ecclesiastes have often become bogged down trying to think their way beyond the literally given instead of first *experiencing* life's paradoxical truth. First-order experience, not second-order critical abstraction, can best unlock the wisdom of this enigmatic book. This we have encouraged by way of the stories filmmakers have given us. But the conversation should be two-way. By way of conclusion, therefore, we need to revisit the text critically. We do this both to hear Ecclesiastes speak afresh given the interpretive light of these movies and to let this biblical text address the films with its own voice.

In Ecclesiastes, Qoheleth offers his understanding of life. He looks closely at this world and sees the following.

Death is our common fate. It is not true that the wise person always possesses life and the fool always possesses death, as some sages might teach. Death is the great leveler. Writes Qoheleth, "The living should always remind themselves that death is waiting for us all" (7:2; cf. 2:14–16; 3:18–21; 5:12–17; 6:6; 7:2–4; 8:8; 9:2–6; 12:1–7). Our mortality strikes terror in our hearts, for life is precious. And so we often live in denial. But though death calls into question life's very meaning, it also reminds us of the wonder of life. This is our experience in watching *American Beauty.* This is Watanabe's experience too *(Ikiru).* Perhaps, the visible graveyard helps Leticia break the cycle of anger and violence and accept the gift of shared life with Hank *(Monster's Ball).*

We cannot know what we are to do. Life is inscrutable, indiscernible, mysterious. All human plans fail, not only because death frustrates them but also because the regularity of life eludes our grasp. Qoheleth asks rhetorically, "How can anyone know what is best for us in this short, useless life of ours—a life that passes like a shadow?" (6:12; cf. 5:9; 7:23–24; 10:14; 11:5). There is a right time for everything, yet we experience grief and frustration, for we cannot really know what time that is (cf. 3:1–12). Warren Schmidt cannot figure out how best to respond to his daughter's marriage to Randall *(About Schmidt).*

Philippa is wrongly convinced that Turin's drug lord must be stopped at any price *(Heaven)*. Lola runs, but . . . *(Run Lola Run)*.

Life lacks any discernible moral order. Life too often seems random. Life does not evidence any sense of justice or appropriate retribution. The good sometimes lose everything; the evil at times prosper. The selfless act goes unnoticed. Even when good is exhibited, one rotten apple spoils the barrel. "Look at what happens in the world," Qoheleth observes. "Sometimes the righteous get the punishment of the wicked, and the wicked get the reward of the righteous" (8:14; cf. 3:16; 4:1–3; 5:8; 7:15–18; 9:11). Ben goes blind, while Judah can "forget" his crime and move on with life *(Crimes and Misdemeanors)*. Lester is shot just as his life comes together *(American Beauty)*. Graham Hess cannot understand the random accident that claimed the life of his wife *(Signs)*.

In short, life is messy. Even Qoheleth's style of argument demonstrates this fact: His short book lacks straightforwardness or progression. Form follows content. The Book of Ecclesiastes doubles back on itself, picking up life's contradictory elements. Wisdom is both useless and better than foolishness. Life is pointless and yet precious. We are to enjoy life's gift yet recognize that it is vain. What the writer gives us with his right hand, he often takes back with his left. After all, Qoheleth recognizes, "How can anyone straighten out what God has made crooked?" (7:13; cf. 1:14–15). In *Crimes and Misdemeanors,* the rabbi goes blind yet is happy, and the murderer goes scot-free and is also happy! The sign in *Monster's Ball* says that it has to be someone's fault, but car breakdowns, eviction notices, racial taunts, and the death of Leticia's son go beyond blame—they simply are robbing Leticia of any semblance of life.

Given life's incoherence, all attempts to master life by our own effort are simply futile. "We labor, trying to catch the wind, and what do we get?" (5:16; cf. 2:22–23; 7:16–18; 8:12–14; 9:11). Our work, wisdom, laughter, and riches prove to hold no meaning. "You spend your life working, laboring, and what do you have to show for it?" (1:3; cf. 2:18; 4:4–6). "I discovered that laughter is foolish, that pleasure does you no good" (2:2; cf. 2:4–12). "No one remembers the wise, and no one remembers fools. . . . We must all die—wise and foolish alike" (2:16; cf. 1:13–18). "If you love money, you will never be satisfied; if you long to be rich, you will never get all you want" (5:10). Money (Linda), fame (Jimmy), power (Earl), and wisdom (Stanley, Donnie) do not satisfy the characters in *Magnolia*. Work, spouse, family, heritage—nothing can fill Warren Schmidt's void *(About Schmidt)*. "Eat, drink, and be merry" proves hollow for Watanabe *(Ikiru)*. Even the life of a clergyman seems devoid of meaning for Graham Hess *(Signs)*.

It is best to accept life's small joys as they are offered. There is a sanctity about the ordinary. "All of us should eat and drink and enjoy what we have worked for. It is God's gift" (3:13; cf. 2:24–25; 3:22; 5:18–20; 6:9; 8:15; 9:7–10; 11:7–10). This gift is rooted in creation itself. Throughout his short book, Qoheleth alludes to the creation story in Genesis, where God created humankind and said it was "very good." We are said to be from the dust; light is judged "good"; one's wife is a companion; toil is tiresome; death is tragic; God is sovereign. The old *sensei* in *Madadayo* gathers with his former students each year to once again say yes to life. Lester is overcome by life's simple gifts—the falling leaves, his grandmother's hands, his daughter at Halloween *(American Beauty)*. Claudia can finally smile as Jim offers his gift of love *(Magnolia)*.

Qoheleth invites his readers to look more deeply at life. The verb "to see" (Hebrew, *ra'ah*) is used forty-seven times in his short reflection. Readers are encouraged to see life honestly yet paradoxically—not only in its bleakness and mystery but also as something worthy of enjoyment. "It is good," writes Qoheleth, "to be able to enjoy the pleasant light of day. Be grateful for every year you live. No matter how long you live, remember that you will be dead much longer" (11:7). The bank guard might be right that all he can know is that the ball is round and the game is ninety minutes, but Lola's gift of care shows that there is more to life than mere chance and choice *(Run Lola Run)*. Ricky has been shut out from much of life by an overbearing father, but his camcorder allows him to look closer and see beneath the surface of life. It leaves him (and his viewers) breathless *(American Beauty)*. April Grace provides Frank the opportunity to look again at his dysfunctional family, and the result is a deeper "grace" *(Magnolia)*.

What Qoheleth offers is an alternate form of wisdom, one that both corrects and recenters the dominant wisdom of his day. Life too easily becomes a project to be managed, a problem to be solved. Wisdom is too easily reduced to a formula by which life can be navigated. The Book of Proverbs teaches, "When a fool speaks, he is ruining himself; he gets caught in the trap of his own words" (18:7). While a valid generalization, it is also true that some fools prosper despite their speech. We cannot turn sage observations into hard-and-fast rules to which even God is beholden. Qoheleth questions such a misuse of Hebraic wisdom. It cannot be turned into a formula for successful living: "Only the wise know what things really mean. Wisdom makes them smile and makes their frowns disappear" (8:1). Leticia understands this, as does Claudia and Bodo, Lester and Warren *(Monster's Ball, Magnolia, The Princess and the Warrior, American Beauty, About Schmidt).*

Finally, for Qoheleth, life is a divine gift. All life is rooted in and dependent on God for its ongoingness and favor. Qoheleth is absolutely clear on this—clearer, in fact, than many of the filmmakers (the exceptions might be M. Night Shyamalan and Alan Ball). Qoheleth's God may be detected not so much by sight as by scent and footprint, but he is unquestionably present nonetheless. Scholars have sometimes missed this important foundation for Ecclesiastes, believing the book to be secular in its orientation. But this is a mistake. It is true that Qoheleth uses the generic term for God, Elohim, rather than the more personal and distinctively Hebraic name, Yahweh. It is true that God is perceived as distant. But according to Qoheleth, God makes everything (11:5)—the beautiful (3:11 NIV) and the crooked (7:13), the good and the bad times (7:14). He gives humankind the days of their lives (5:18; 8:15), their spirit, or breath (12:7), their work (5:19–20), their wealth (5:19; 6:2), and their sustenance (2:24–26; 5:19). He also gives burdens (1:13; 3:10). God tests people (3:18) and will judge (11:9), taking no pleasure in fools (5:4) and calling the past into account (3:14). Though clearly present in all of life, God is also incomprehensible to Qoheleth. God is in heaven, and we are on earth (5:2). We cannot know what he has done (3:11).

Qoheleth's understanding of God, therefore, reveals the same paradox as does his understanding of life. God is present yet absent. He gives meaning to life yet is incomprehensible. He makes both the beautiful and the burdensome. Believers, whether Jewish or Christian, have questioned for centuries why God's gracious personal presence is not more evident in Qoheleth's text. But such is sometimes the reality of life. We too sometimes cry out for God's presence, given his absence. Given external circumstances that cause us to question life, we can either harden our hearts or look for faint motions of grace.[7] Qoheleth chooses the latter, looking at what is close at hand—one's food and drink, one's companions and work—to uncover the presence of God's Spirit. He finds God's footprint to be present, even in life's darkest moments. Neither death nor life's amorality nor life's ongoing mystery can cancel out his belief in God's sustaining presence. They, in fact, somehow compel it.

This was also the experience of Ricky *(American Beauty),* and so too Graham Hess *(Signs).* Perhaps this was the faint experience of Lola *(Run Lola Run)* and of Warren Schmidt *(About Schmidt).* Locating God in the midst of life's pain is not limited to the text and the screen, however. It is also our experience as readers and viewers. After viewing the ending of *Magnolia,* for example, where Jim offers his unconditional love to Claudia and she miraculously responds with a faint smile, one of my students said that that moment was for him a "divine encounter." The fact that the director kept Jim out of the frame for much of the scene while his voice bestowed grace on Claudia allowed the scene to transcend its particular and become a conversation between this student and the divine. The movie served as a catalyst for his "return to faith after a decade of apostasy." The motions of grace reach out as life encounters life.

A Concluding Reflection

A newspaper article in the summer of 2003 titled "Losers on the Rise" chronicled the role of the antihero in a growing number of recent movies. "Unhip, unhandsome, depressed and depressing," these new antiheroes are a far cry from Paul Newman as "Cool

Hand Luke" or the Jack Nicholson of *Five Easy Pieces*. Wrote the author, "The latest incarnation of the antihero is . . . neither tough nor sexual; he's an everyday schlump who rejects conventional ideas of romance, success and even basic grooming. Unhappy, depressed, confused, he slouches through life, in places such as Omaha or Cleveland, sometimes mocking traditionalists."[8]

Lester Burnham and Warren Schmidt were two of the author's case studies. Deeply flawed and not necessarily redeemed, these antiheroes defy conventional values. They recognize life's meaninglessness, even if they have no meaningful project to substitute. They end up "clinging to the thinnest of things." Yet these characters also have an appealing defiance, a sweet sadness.

The writer quoted Ray Carney, the film studies director at Boston University. Carney questions such antiheroes on ethical grounds. "If you actually bought into the ironic view, you'd be paralyzed. It's not an adult view you can live by. [Antihero] films allow for mocking at what it is but not telling you what is the next step. It's a complicated thing. It's not entirely good to be in the antihero situation. It raises the troubling questions of how do you live your life, how do you go on from there?"[9]

But there is an alternate way to view such irony. Carney misses the possibility that what is mocked is what has proven falsely Pollyanna. Life sometimes simply presents itself in its absurdity; the antihero is not a cinematic artifice, an invention in life. Instead, he often represents our lives to us. There are "ordinary people," writes Lewis Smedes, who are "too weak to cope with the terrible stuff . . . non-heroes—not cowards . . . people who live on the edge . . . who cry for a sign, any old sign, that it might still be all right even when everything seems horribly wrong."[10] Here is Qoheleth, the writer of Ecclesiastes—and Lester Burnham and Ricky Fitts, Jim Kurring and Phil Parma, Leticia Musgrove and Hank Grotowski. Here, as well, are Warren and Sissi, Lola and Graham.

September 11, 2001, did not create the recognition that beauty must be found within the terrible or not at all. It did, however, deepen the perception. All is not well with our world. The creation groans. And yet Ricky's confession to Jane is also true. As he recalled the "thinnest of things," a plastic bag dancing in the wind, he could say with a sincerity that revealed the screenwriter's heart, "That's the day I realized there was this entire life behind things, and this incredibly benevolent force that wanted me to know there was no reason to be afraid . . . ever." Here is Qoheleth's hard-won observation as well. Death's nonsense might still prevail. Grace and virtue might turn into stupidity. But there is a fugitive energy, divinely given, that propels life forward even in the darkest of days. Its useless beauty might leave some things unanswered, but its reality should never be disparaged.

APPENDIX A

ECCLESIASTES' HISTORY OF INTERPRETATION

Medieval Old Testament scholars called Ecclesiastes one of the Bible's "two dangerous books." (The other was the Song of Songs with its overt sensuality.) Though its trenchant observations on life revealed a fragile joy—a useless beauty—its paragraphs also brimmed over with a cynicism and even despair that seemed out of place in the Bible's grand narrative. Biblical scholars have tried various "solutions" to mitigate Ecclesiastes' "danger." The first thousand years of Christian interpretation saw the negative conclusions of Ecclesiastes as support for asceticism and discipline, encouragement to despise the things of the world and to turn, instead, to the immortality of the next life. The book's commendations to enjoy one's food and drink were given an allegorical interpretation: The advice referred to the joy associated with partaking of Christ's body and blood in the sacrament.

Martin Luther and the Reformers later challenged such an otherworldly interpretation, finding this *via negativa* rooted more in the medieval contempt for this life than in the biblical text itself. They believed Qoheleth's purpose in writing the book was to demonstrate humankind's depraved affections. According to the Reformers, Ecclesiastes showed the vanity, or futility, of life "under the sun"—that is, outside God's saving grace. Ecclesiastes explored the consequences and bankruptcy of secular thinking. The book served as the "question" for which the New Testament gospel provided the "answer." Again, an outside factor, Luther's concentration on salvation by grace, proved determinative in arriving at the book's meaning.

According to modern criticism, these traditional interpretations of Ecclesiastes were unsatisfying in regard to the text as text. They also did not address the paradoxical nature of the book. Scholars found in this short book not only negation but also affirmation, not only despair but also wonder, not only a focus on life under the sun but also a focus on God's transcendent judgment and grace. New interpretive strategies were needed. In keeping with modernity's commitment to rationality and logical coherence, most commentators concentrated on leveling out the inconsistencies found within the book. They tried to make Qoheleth's paradoxical thought fit into a more systematic mind-set. After all, a writer could not say one thing and then its opposite in the same breath.

Some interpreters hypothesized that in the course of making an argument, Qoheleth quoted material with which he did not agree. Thus, the seeming contradictions. Or perhaps later editors interpolated into the text additional material to make the text's radical ideas more palatable. As before, the strategy involved looking for an outside influence to render the text meaningful. But as a recent critic rhetorically asks, "Whether the 'Qohelet' we are left with is anyone other than the product of our own limited imagination is, however, an important question."[1]

More recent interpreters have moved away from reconstructing the text but have been equally vexed by the perceived incoherence of the argument. They have, therefore, tried to smooth out the contradictions by underemphasizing the passages in Ecclesiastes that do not fit into their schema. As a result, they have been able to conclude that Qoheleth was a pessimistic skeptic (James Crenshaw), a practical atheist (Douglas Stuart), or an existential sage who demonstrated life's absurdity (Michael Fox).[2] A few have argued the other side: Despite the fact that life has its enigmas, for Qoheleth there is only one possible attitude to adopt—enjoy what life gives (Graham Ogden).[3]

The book's paradoxical understanding of life, however—one that finds real joy within life's enigmas—calls such undialectical interpretations into question. Too many loose ends remain in the text. The obvious pleasures in life that Qoheleth counsels his readers to enjoy are not so much muted (cf. Roland Murphy)[4] as they are experienced within life's ongoing messiness. Common to all one-sided interpretations, it seems, is the same desire to make the book into "a unified, logically argued and constructed whole."[5]

What that "constructed whole" looks like has continued, of course, to be a matter of debate. Resigned? Realistic? Fatalistic? A critical corrective? One scholar, after surveying recent studies on Ecclesiastes, summarized her findings: "A hallmark of Qoheleth studies is the inability of readers to agree on the central message and tonality [or atonality] of the book."[6] Why is this? Another scholar perceptively concluded that "very different types have found their own image in Ecclesiastes. . . . There are many aspects in our book; different interpreters have highlighted what was most fitting for themselves and their age, and they understood it in their own way. But for all there was a difficulty, namely, that there were also other aspects which could hardly be harmonized with their preferred view."[7]

Jacques Ellul, the French sociologist and lay theologian who wrote a book on Ecclesiastes after reading and reflecting on the text for over fifty years, perceptively summarized the problem with interpretations of Ecclesiastes:

> Qoheleth proposes an idea that is more than modern: he does not consider disorder, nonsense, incoherence, and contradiction as accidents, like an evil we must eliminate, some secondary or chance event. Instead, he treats these elements as inherent in human social life. He integrates disorder and contradiction into humanity's "normal" being. This is simply extraordinary.
>
> Because of this view, Qoheleth has been rejected and left out, or interpreted in a moralizing, normalizing sense, to make him

conform to the "norm." The norm of human life was order, peace, noncontradiction, reconciliation, and all sorts of laws (moral, natural, political, and later scientific). It was regularity, consistency, and harmony. So perturbation and disorder seemed abnormal: "accidents" to be eliminated at all costs. Fortuitous tendencies had to be reduced and clarified.[8]

It is this interpretive history that greets readers of Ecclesiastes today. Thus, it is not surprising that much of its interpretation is still couched in negative terms. But something new is also emerging within our postmodern culture, in which paradox and contradiction are no longer as easily excluded. The contemporary mind-set, mirrored in the films just considered, is providing new glasses through which to see Ecclesiastes. And the result is proving helpful. The present book is one example of a new trend in Ecclesiastes scholarship. It seeks to provide a narrative context in which life's uselessness and its God-given beauty might be concurrently embraced.

APPENDIX B

CHRISTIAN FILM CRITICISM

Film criticism from a Christian viewpoint is a difficult genre to describe. Some Christian movie critics offer a content analysis of movies as to their moral suitability (read this as the presence, or lack thereof, of sex, violence, coarse language, or a pagan worldview). Although this largely oppositional approach to secular culture is perhaps more typical of previous eras, it is still practiced and is what the secular press often sees as synonymous with "Christian" criticism.

A recent book by Ted Baehr, for example, criticized the first Harry Potter movie for its "occult, pagan worldview" while giving high praise to *Left Behind* and *Jurassic Park III*.[1] Parents needing a way to screen what their preteens see might be helped by such reviews (though not in the case of his caution regarding *Harry Potter*, in which the occult is not the point). But most contemporary movie fans, whether Christian or not, are uncomfortable with such one-dimensional evaluations. (Should we really caution adolescent and adult viewers against seeing *Schindler's List* or *Amistad* because of the nudity and violence?)

The approach too often ends up pitting Christian "judgment" (or the lack thereof) against both what the average viewer experiences as significant and what film critics find on artistic grounds to be excellent cinema. Thankfully, a growing number of other approaches to Christianity and film criticism have appeared in the last decade and have largely supplanted such reactionary responses.

A small but growing number of Christian scholars have entered the academic arena, offering reflection on selected films, much as a previous generation of scholars of religion attempted to bring issues of faith and literary scholarship together.[2] Younger Christian critics have also begun, in more postmodern terms, to offer their personal and irreverent reflections on faith and film in the hope of encouraging their peers who both love film and love God.[3]

Others have attempted, through Christian film criticism, to serve the institutional church more directly by providing it with resources for varied use. Some of these books correlate films with the liturgy for the church year;[4] others identify film clips as illustrative material for Christian youth ministry;[5] and still others seek to provide Christian study groups with resources for discussion and teaching.[6] Additional books seek to provide resources for deepening one's spirituality[7] and for educating Christians in their faith by correlating theological topics, creeds, or worldviews with selected movies.[8] Common to all is the attempt to find parallels or points of discussion between movie portrayals and Christian life and thought. There is a vital place for such criticism, as the increased use of media in churches suggests. When done well, this genre provides a dialogue between faith and film that is instructive to both.

But there is yet another approach to Christian faith and film that the present book represents and seeks to extend. Larry Kreitzer, in his series of books on literature, film, and Scripture, attempts to reverse the hermeneutical flow.[9] In other words, rather than move from sacred text to literature and film in the act of understanding, Kreitzer proposes that we move in the opposite direction, from film to sacred text. Robert Jewett works similarly but prefers to label his approach "an interpretive arch."[10] What both are suggesting, despite their differences, is that movies can help Christian readers of the biblical text better understand what they are reading.

This book has sought to extend their provocative suggestion by exploring its relevance with regard to the Book of Ecclesiastes. In doing so, it has commented indirectly on several of the other approaches to Christian criticism. For example, almost all the movies discussed in this volume are R-rated movies. Given Ecclesiastes' basic themes—life's vanity, death, amorality, our existence's inscrutability—it should not be surprising that movies that correlate with this hard-edged book come with a rough veneer. But if, in fact, such R-rated movies can help faithful readers understand the biblical text in ways they otherwise might miss, then much of Christian film criticism must be critiqued for being too cautious. It has tended to base its judgments only on "truth" already understood and has limited its range of movies to those with more "uplifting" themes.

The challenge for the Christian is the same as that for any religious film critic: Can the conversation between faith and culture be a robust one that actually goes both ways? That is, can culture be instructive to faith, not just vice versa? This is the experience of growing numbers of filmgoers who are also men and women of faith. Hollywood is informing the church and the church, Hollywood.

APPENDIX C

BIBLICAL CRITICISM AND *USELESS BEAUTY*

When seeking to understand a piece of literature, critics have long recognized that in addition to considering the text itself (e.g., *Hamlet*), one should also pay attention to the mind-set of the author who wrote the text (Shakespeare and his world), the person who reads the text (a twenty-first-century student who might already have seen a movie version of it), and the view of the world embedded in the text ("To be or not to be. That is the question.").[1] A full-orbed criticism would, of course, be cognizant of all these questions and concerns, but where one begins and what approaches are thought to have greater usefulness necessarily shape one's final interpretation. This is as true of biblical studies as of literary criticism more generally.

Scholars working in the field of biblical studies have noted that in differing eras the focus of attention has been placed on all four points of this literary-critical circle with predictably different interpretive results.[2] Precritical biblical scholarship, for example, focused on the fact that the Bible was theology—it was *theo/logos,* God's

Word. The *words* of the text needed to be interpreted, therefore, by the *Word.* Through much of the twentieth century, the interpreter's attention shifted to the author and his world. Scholarly attention focused on the historical context of God's Word as human words. Who was the author of the biblical text? How did he compose his book? What was the context in which he wrote? Who was his audience? And so on. More recently, literary criticism has been used to turn critical attention back to the very words of the text itself. Scholars have attempted to understand not so much who edited a text as how the final shape of the edited text influences our understanding of it. New ways of studying texts have thus been applied to reading the Scriptures. What rhetorical devices are present? What difference does it make that it is a narrative, for example? As we have entered the postmodern era, scholars have adopted more and more a fourth methodology, a reader-response approach to biblical criticism. They have noted, for example, how women might identify with a different aspect in a particular text than men, or how Latin Americans might identify with a different aspect than those in the United States.

What is true of biblical studies more generally is also true with regard to the interpretation of the Book of Ecclesiastes. Premoderns, disturbed by Qoheleth's theology, often focused on the sage's depiction of "life under the sun." They believed the book described life without God. Ecclesiastes, therefore, needed to be completed by the theology of the rest of the Bible. Modern biblical scholars turned their attention first to historical-critical concerns (Given the seeming contradictions in the text, were there multiple authors? What were the Greek influences on the book?) and more recently to literary ones (Might the author have made use of quotations that were then refuted? Is the book ironic? Can one perceive a narrative shape?). Occasionally, scholarly work on Ecclesiastes has ventured into reader-oriented criticism, as when existentialist theologians found in Ecclesiastes existentialist themes (see chap. 2).

But Carol Newsom has noted rightly "that scholarly work on Ecclesiastes has remained, with very few exceptions, the province of traditional historical criticism."[3] Of commentaries written in the last twenty-five years, for example, only two or three have strongly made use of literary-critical approaches or have turned to the reader as a central critical locus. Interestingly, though this biblical text has a decidedly postmodern ring, little attention has been given to how a reader-oriented approach to the text might help unpack its meaning. Moreover, after years of more sterile critical scholarship, relatively little scholarship has focused on Ecclesiastes as God's Word to its readers.

This small volume has been an attempt both to explore what a reader/viewer-oriented criticism might contribute to an understanding of Ecclesiastes and to recover something of the premodern's concern for hearing God's Word anew. To alter the metaphor, it has sought to put contemporary film into dialogue with the Book of Ecclesiastes to help us "see the voice of the Lord."

NOTES

Preface

1. For an introduction to Christian film criticism, see Robert K. Johnston, *Reel Spirituality: Theology and Film in Dialogue* (Grand Rapids: Baker Academic, 2000).

2. One thinks of such fine books as William Romanowski, *Eyes Wide Open* (Grand Rapids: Brazos, 2001); and Brian Godawa, *Hollywood Worldviews: Watching Films with Wisdom and Discernment* (Downers Grove, Ill.: InterVarsity, 2002).

3. Two critics who have done helpful work in reversing "the hermeneutical flow" are Larry Kreitzer and Robert Jewett (see chap. 1 for a discussion of their work).

Chapter 1

1. Elvis Costello, "All This Useless Beauty," from Elvis Costello and the Attractions, *All This Useless Beauty* (Warner Brothers Records, 1996).

2. I owe this observation to my friend J. Walker Smith.

3. The term *Qoheleth* means "the one who assembles" (people? ideas?) and has sometimes been mistakenly translated "the preacher."

4. "The discomfort of the community of biblical faith with Ecclesiastes is not, however, a new phenomenon. From the very beginning, it is evident that the nature of the book itself as authoritative Scripture was doubted by a significant number of Jews. Two famous passages in the Mishnah, echoed in the Talmud and in later Jewish writings, refer to disputes among the rabbis on precisely this point—whether or not Ecclesiastes 'defiles the hands.' They make clear that this issue divided the famous rabbinic schools of Hillel (which thought it did defile the hands) and Shammai (which thought it did not)" (Ian Provan, *Ecclesiastes, Song of Songs,* The NIV Application Commentary [Grand Rapids: Zondervan, 2001], 23).

5. Quoted in Daniel Pawley, "Ecclesiastes—Reaching Out to the Twentieth Century," *Bible Review* 6, no. 5 (October 1990): 34–36. Pawley also provides the other references in this paragraph except for U2.

6. U2, "The Wanderer," *Zooropa* (UMVD Jumpstart, 1993).

7. John B. Ravenal, *Vanitas: Meditations on Life and Death in Contemporary Art* (Richmond: Virginia Museum of Fine Arts, 2000), 13.

8. See appendix C.

9. Larry Kreitzer, *The New Testament in Fiction and Film: On Reversing the Hermeneutical Flow* (Sheffield: JSOT Press, 1993); idem, *The Old Testament in Fiction and Film: On Reversing the Hermeneutical Flow* (Sheffield: JSOT Press, 1994); idem, *Pauline Images in Fiction and Film: On Reversing the Hermeneutical Flow* (Sheffield: JSOT Press, 1999); and idem, *Gospel Images in Fiction and Film: On Reversing the Hermeneutical Flow* (Sheffield: JSOT Press, 2002).

10. Philip Yancey, *The Jesus I Never Knew* (Grand Rapids: Zondervan, 1995).

11. Robert Jewett, *St. Paul Returns to the Movies: Triumph over Shame* (Grand Rapids: Eerdmans, 1999), 20. See also idem, *St. Paul at the Movies: The Apostle's Dialogue with American Culture* (Louisville: Westminster John Knox, 1993).

12. Jeremy Begbie, "Through Music: Sound Mix," in *Beholding the Glory: Incarnation through the Arts,* ed. Jeremy Begbie (Grand Rapids: Baker, 2000). Cf. Jeremy S. Begbie, *Theology, Music, and Time* (Cambridge: Cambridge University Press, 2000).

13. Cf. Roland Murphy, *Ecclesiastes,* Word Biblical Commentary 23A (Dallas: Word, 1992), 27: "But it is difficult to find more than the mood of a resigned conclusion in such passages. There are not recommendations that Qoheleth truly finds joy in. He can only offer them in a mysterious and incalculable world: What else can one do?"

14. "Biblical Worldview and Evangelical Theological Education," a report of the Wilburforce Forum Seminary Fellows (2003).

15. Jürgen Moltmann, *The Spirit of Life: A Universal Affirmation* (Minneapolis: Fortress, 1992), 8.

16. See Robert K. Johnston, "Rethinking Common Grace: Toward a Theology of Co-Relation," in *Grace upon Grace,* ed. Robert K. Johnston, L. Gregory Jones, and Jonathan R. Wilson (Nashville: Abingdon, 1999), 153–68.

17. Elizabeth Barrett Browning, *Aurora Leigh* (New York: Penguin, 1996), book 7.

18. I also wish to pay homage to Ecclesiastes, which has fascinated me since as a high school student I gave my first public speech based on the book's advice. My first published article as a young professor just starting out in academia was again on Ecclesiastes, a theological reappraisal of the book that I titled "Confessions of a Workaholic: A Reappraisal of Qoheleth," *Catholic Biblical Quarterly* 38 (1976): 14–28.

19. Gerhard von Rad, *Old Testament Theology,* vol. 1, trans. D. M. G. Stacker (New York: Harper & Row, 1962), 421.

20. Elizabeth Huwiler, "Ecclesiastes," in Roland Murphy and Elizabeth Huwiler, *Proverbs, Ecclesiastes, Song of Songs,* New International Biblical Commentary, Old Testament, vol. 12 (Peabody, Mass.: Hendrickson, 1999), 165.

21. Johnston, "Confessions," 14.

22. Elsa Tamaz, "When Horizons Close: A Reflection on the Utopian Ratio of Qoheleth," in *The Future of Theology,* ed. Miroslav Volf, Carmen Krieg, and Thomas Kucharz (Grand Rapids: Eerdmans, 1996), 217; and Elsa Tamaz, "Living Wisely in the Midst of Absurdity," *Church and Society* 86 (March/April 1996): 35.

23. Interview with Rudolph Gulianni, *Extra,* December 19, 2001.

24. William Rhoden, "While People Die, NCAA Should Stop Its Tournament," *International Herald Tribune,* March 25, 2003, 20.

25. Quoted in Craig Detweiler and Barry Taylor, *A Matrix of Meanings: Finding God in Pop Culture* (Grand Rapids: Baker Academic, 2003), 314.

26. Reed Johnson, "It's All for One," *Los Angeles Times,* December 22, 2002, sec. E, pp. 1, 38.

27. J. Walker Smith, "America.2," privately circulated paper. What follows in this section is largely dependent on Smith's assessment.

28. Ibid.

29. Lewis Smedes, *How Can It Be All Right When Everything Is All Wrong?* (San Francisco: Harper & Row, 1982), 16.

Chapter 2

1. Søren Kierkegaard, *Repetition* (1843), quoted in Nathan A. Scott Jr., *The Unquiet Vision: Mirrors of Man in Existentialism* (New York: Excalibur Books, World Publishing, 1969), 20. In what follows, I am dependent for the general contours of my description on Scott's fine volume as well as on the basic introduction by Roger Shinn, *The Existentialist Posture,* rev. ed. (New York: Association Press, 1970).

2. Scott, *Unquiet Vision,* 187–88.

3. Michael V. Fox, "The Innerstructure of Qohelet's Thought," in *Qohelet in the Context of Wisdom,* ed. A. Schoors (Leuven, Bel.: Leuven University Press, 1998), 226–27.

4. Elizabeth Huwiler, "Ecclesiastes," in Roland Murphy and Elizabeth Huwiler, *Proverbs, Ecclesiastes, Song of Songs,* New International Biblical Commentary, Old Testament, vol. 12 (Peabody, Mass: Hendrickson, 1999), 165.

5. Fox, "Innerstructure of Qohelet's Thought," 227.

6. Cf. Michael V. Fox, *Qohelet and His Contradictions* (Sheffield: Sheffield Academic Press, 1987), 10.

7. Quoted in Rick Lyman, "Akira Kurosawa, Film Director, Is Dead at 88," *New York Times,* September 7, 1998, nytimes.com/search/article.

8. Quoted in Jack Kroll, "Tolstoy with a Camera," *Newsweek,* September 21, 1998, 65.

9. Quoted in Leonard Maltin, *Movie Encyclopedia,* reprinted in "Biography for Akira Kurosawa," International Movie Data Base, imbd.com/Bio?Kurosawa,%20Akira.

10. Quoted in Lyman, "Akira Kurosawa."

11. Barbara Carr, "Goethe and Kurosawa: Faust and the Totality of Human Experience—West and East," *Literature Film Quarterly* 24, no. 3 (1996): 274.

12. Quoted in "Biography for Akira Kurosawa."

13. Quoted in Donald Richie, ed., *Ikiru: A Film by Akira Kurosawa* (New York: Simon & Schuster, 1968), 6.

14. Ibid., 7.

15. Ibid., 10.

16. David Desser, "*Ikiru:* Narration as a Moral Act," in *Reframing Japanese Cinema,* ed. Arthur Nolletti Jr. and David Desser (Bloomington: Indiana University Press, 1992), 65.

17. Ibid., 67. Desser might better have turned to another existentialist, Albert Camus, to make his same point. After struggling with whether our experience of the world as absurd means that everything is permitted, Camus concluded that our neighbor's right also to rebel limits our rebellion against the absurd. Thus, no action detrimental to our fellow humanity can be allowed. Such an action would side with the absurd against humans. See, for example, Camus, *The Plague* (1947) and *The Rebel* (1951).

18. Quoted in Stig Bjorkman, *Woody Allen on Woody Allen* (New York: Grove Press, 1993), 211.

19. Quoted in Eric Lax, *Woody Allen: A Biography* (New York: Random House, 1991), 225.

20. Mark Roche, "Justice and the Withdrawal of God in Woody Allen's *Crimes and Misdemeanors,*" *Journal of Value Inquiry* 29 (December 1995): 562.

21. Woody Allen, quoted in Bjorkman, *Woody Allen on Woody Allen,* 223.

22. Ibid., 210.

23. Ibid., 225.

24. For a helpful discussion, see Crystal Downing, "Woody Allen's Blindness and Insight: The Palimpsets of *Crimes and Misdemeanors,*" *Religion and the Arts* 1, no. 2 (spring 1997): 87, 90.

25. Eugene Borowitz, "Heeding Ecclesiastes, at Long Last" in "Woody Allen Counts the Wages of Sin," *New York Times,* October 15, 1989, 16.

Chapter 3

1. Quoted in Kathleen Norris, "Turning from Beauty: A Life Lived in Sight of the End Is the Truest Life of All," *Forbes ASAP Supplement* 166, no. 9 (October 2, 2000): 253.

2. Jay Carr, "'Beauty' Is Biting Look at Roses," *Boston Globe,* September 17, 1999, www.rottentomatoes.com/m/AmericanBeauty-1093536.

3. Quoted in Bob Longino, "'Beauty' Maker," *Atlanta Journal-Constitution,* March 26, 2000, sec. L, p. 4.

4. Karl Rahner, quoted in Norris, "Turning from Beauty," 253.

5. Quoted in Robert J. Elisberg, "E-mail Interview with Alan Ball," www. written by.com/craft/interviews/ball.html.

6. Alan Ball, "My Perspective: Beauty and the Box Office," *Advocate* no. 808 (March 28, 2000): 11.

7. Marc Peyser, "Six Feet under Our Skin," *Newsweek,* March 18, 2002, 52.

8. Quoted in ibid., 54–55.

9. Quoted in ibid., 57.

Chapter 4

1. Quoted in Lynn Hirschberg, "His Way," *New York Times Magazine* (December 1999): 1, www.ptanderson.com/articlesandinterviews/nytimesmagazine.html.

2. Quoted in Patrick Goldstein, "The New New Wave, *Los Angeles Times,* December 12, 1999, 5–6, www.ptanderson.com/articlesandinterviews/latimes2.htm.

3. Interview with Chris Garcia, "All Paul Thomas Anderson Does," Austin360 .com, January 6, 2000, www.austin360.com/entertainment/xl/cinema/2000/01/ 06cinema_003.html.

4. Ibid., 2.

5. Quoted in "Production Notes," www.magnoliamovie.com/infoMIDprod .html.

6. Neal Gabler, *Life the Movie: How Entertainment Conquered Reality* (New York: Knopf, 1998).

7. Quoted in Mark Olsen, "Singing in the Rain," *Sight and Sound* 10, no. 3 (March 2000): 28.

8. Paul Thomas Anderson, *Magnolia: The Shooting Script* (New York: Newmarket Press, 2000), 198.

9. Quoted in Olsen, "Singing in the Rain," 28.

10. Quoted in Gavin Smith, "Night Fever," *Sight and Sound* 8, no. 1 (January 1998): 6–11.

11. For a perceptive discussion of Anderson's use of music in *Boogie Nights,* see Kelly Ritter, "Spectacle at the Disco," *Journal of Popular Film & Television* 28, no. 4 (winter 2001): 166–75.

12. Quoted in Roger Ebert, "'Love' at First Sight," *Chicago Sun Times,* October 13, 2002, sec. SHOW, p. 1.

13. Roger Ebert, "Magnolia," *Chicago Sun Times,* January 2000, www. suntimes .com/ebert/ebert_reviews/2000/01/010701.html.

14. Moira Macdonald, "Director Now 'Punch Drunk' over Comedy," *Seattle Times,* October 13, 2002, sec. L, p. 6.

15. Quoted in "Production Notes," *Magnolia* official website, www.magnolia movie.com/infoMIDprod.html.

Chapter 5

1. Quoted in Cynthia Fuchs, "Interview with Tom Tykwer and Franka Potente," www.popmatters.com/film/interviews/princess-warrior.html.

2. Quoted in "Interview with Tom Tykwer and Franka Potente," June 8, 2001, www.themoviechicks.com/jul2001/mcrtprincess.html.

3. For a helpful discussion of third wave German cinema, see Wade Major, "Reunified, Revitalized," *Los Angeles Times,* September 22, 2002, calendar section, 8, 72.

4. Quoted in Demetrios Matheou, "Dead Man Talking," *Observer,* April 21, 2002, 9.

5. Quoted in Katherine Monk, "Heaven 'about Freeing the Spirit of Your Mind,'" *Vancouver Sun,* October 30, 2002, sec. C, p. 7.

6. Quoted in Duane Dudek, "German Director of 'The Princess and the Warrior' Finds His Niche," *Milwaukee Journal Sentinel,* July 13, 2001, Entertainment News.

7. "Commentary by Director, Writer, and Producer Tom Tykwer and Actress Franka Potente," *Run Lola Run* DVD (Sony, 1999).

8. Quoted in Anthony Kaufman, "Interview: Run Tykwer Run; From Lola to 'The Princess and the Warrior,'" IndieWIRE, www.indiewire.com/film/interviews/int_Tykwer_Tom_010625.html.

9. See Tom Beaudoin, *Virtual Faith: The Irreverent Spiritual Quest of Generation X* (San Francisco: Jossey-Bass, 1998).

10. Paul Tillich, *Systematic Theology,* vol. 1 (Chicago: University of Chicago Press, 1951), 83–86; cf. Paul Tillich, *Systematic Theology,* vol. 3 (Chicago: University of Chicago Press, 1963), 249–68.

11. Elizabeth Huwiler, "Ecclesiastes," in Roland Murphy and Elizabeth Huwiler, *Proverbs, Ecclesiastes, and Song of Songs,* New International Biblical Commentary, Old Testament, vol. 12 (Peabody, Mass.: Hendrickson, 1999), 165.

Chapter 6

1. Billy Bob Thornton, interview, *Dateline NBC,* January 18, 2002.

2. Quoted in Dennis Harvey, "Directors," *Daily Variety,* January 15, 2002, sec. 1, p. A18.

3. Cf. Gary Arnold, "'Monster's Ball' Prurient, Uninspiring: Redemptive Flick Lacks Redemption," *Washington Times,* February 8, 2002, sec. B, p. 6.

4. Quoted in Jeffrey Overstreet, "Film Forum: Violent Movies, Violent Reviews," *Christianity Today Magazine,* February 11, 2002, www.christianity today.com/ct2002/105/43.0.html.

5. Norbert Lohfink, *The Christian Meaning of the Old Testament* (Milwaukee: Bruce, 1968), 148.

6. John Updike, foreword to *Wolfgang Amadeus Mozart,* by Karl Barth (Grand Rapids: Eerdmans, 1986), 11.

7. Karl Barth, *Church Dogmatics,* III/3, *The Doctrine of Creation,* ed. G. W. Bromiley and T. F. Torrance (Edinburgh: T & T Clark, 1961), 298.

Chapter 7

1. Peter Travers, review of *Signs, RollingStone*, quoted on www.rottentomatoes
.com/m/Signs-1114791/.

2. Jeff Giles, "Out of This World," *Newsweek*, August 5, 2002, 51.

3. Maltbie D. Babcock, "This Is My Father's World."

4. Rose Pacatte, review of *Signs*, www.daughtersofstpaul.com/mediastudies/
reviews/filmsigns.html.

5. James Newton Howard, "Reaching the Audience," *The Sixth Sense* Collector's
Edition DVD (Buena Vista, 2002).

6. M. Night Shyamalan, "A Conversation with M. Night Shyamalan," *The Sixth
Sense* Collector's Edition DVD.

7. Quoted by Larry Fine (*Reuters Entertainment*, August 1, 2002), in Dick Staub,
"Seekers on Journey," *Culturewatch*, www.dickstaub.com.

8. Richard Leonard, "Signs," Film Reviews, Australian Catholic Bishops Conference, www.catholic.org.au/film/2002/signs.htm.

9. Jeffrey Overstreet, "Signs, a Third-Draft Review," *Looking Closer Review*, 2002,
promontoryartists.org/lookingcloser/movie%20reviews/Q-Z/signs.htm.

10. Roy Anker, "Signs and Wonders," *Books & Culture* 8, no. 6 (November/
December 2002): 7.

11. These summary judgments are taken from Jeffrey Overstreet's compendium
of Christian film reviewers, "Film Forum: Signs of Faith on the Big Screen," August
8, 2002, www.christianitytoday.com/ct/2002/130/41.0.html.

12. Dick Staub, "Movies: Signs," August 2, 2002, dickstaub.com/culturewatch
.php?record_id=148.

13. Jacques Ellul, *Reason for Being: A Meditation on Ecclesiastes*, trans. Joyce Main
Hanks (Grand Rapids: Eerdmans, 1990), 213.

Chapter 8

1. Quoted in John Hodgman, "The Bard of Omaha," *New York Times Magazine*,
December 8, 2002, query.nytimes.com/search/restricted/article?res=F70E15FE345
C0C7B8CDDAB0994.

2. Anna Bahney, "36 Hours in Omaha," *New York Times*, October 24, 2003, offered
readers an Alexander Payne "driving tour of the cinematic centerpieces of his version of the
middle-class Midwest." The tour starts at the thirty-story Woodmen of the World tower,
travels west to the Dairy Queen where Schmidt ordered a Blizzard, moves on to Schmidt's
home in an area called Happy Hollow, takes a spin past the American Family Inn featured
in *Election*, and ends up at an intersection that Payne uses in all three of his movies.

3. Quoted in ibid.

4. The building functions in the movie almost as a tower of Babel, a monument
to human wisdom that proves to be folly.

5. Roger Ebert, "About Schmidt," *Chicago Sun Times*, December 20, 2002, www
.suntimes.com/ebert/ebert_reviews/2002/12/122001.html.

6. Quoted in "About Schmidt," *Plugged'n Film Reviews,* www.family.org/pplace/pi/films/a0024057.html.

7. Cf. A. O. Scott, "That Mythic American Hero: The Regular Guy," *New York Times Magazine,* December 8, 2002, query.nytimes.com/search/restricted/article?res=F20A14F63C5F0C7B8CDDAB099.

8. Robert K. Johnston, "'Confessions of a Workaholic': A Reappraisal of Qoheleth," *Catholic Biblical Quarterly* 38 (1976): 14–28.

9. See Walter Brueggemann, *In Man We Trust: The Neglected Side of Biblical Faith* (Atlanta: John Knox, 1972); and Gerhard von Rad, *Wisdom in Israel* (Nashville: Abingdon, 1972).

10. Walter Brueggemann, "Scripture and an Ecumenical Life-Style," *Interpretation* 24 (1970): 14.

11. Brueggemann, *In Man We Trust,* 23.

12. Gerhard von Rad, *Wisdom in Israel,* trans. J. D. Martin (New York: Abingdon, 1972), 308, 316.

13. See Robert K. Johnston, *Life Is Not Work, Work Is Not Life* (Berkeley: Wildcat Canyon Press, 2001).

Chapter 9

1. Shelby Coffey, the former editor of the *Los Angeles Times* and *U.S. News & World Report,* kept this cartoon with him for years.

2. The provocative phrase is from Don Saliers, "Where Beauty and Terror Lie: The Poetics of Everyday Life" (The Seventh Distinguished Faculty Lecture, Emory University, Atlanta, March 21, 2002).

3. Ibid.

4. Dietrich Bonhoeffer, *Letters and Papers from Prison,* ed. Eberhard Bethge (New York: Macmillan, 1971), 156–57.

5. Ibid., 166.

6. Ibid., 169.

7. Readers might also find interesting Robert K. Johnston, "John Updike's Theological World," *Christian Century,* November 16, 1977, 1061–66.

8. Lynn Smith, "Losers on the Rise," *Los Angeles Times,* August 17, 2003, sec. E, pp. 1, 26–27.

9. Ibid., 27.

10. Lewis Smedes, *How Can It Be All Right When Everything Is All Wrong?* (San Francisco: Harper & Row, 1962), 79.

Appendix A

1. Ian Provan, *Ecclesiastes, Song of Songs,* The NIV Application Commentary (Grand Rapids: Zondervan, 2001), 32.

2. James Crenshaw, *Ecclesiastes,* Old Testament Library (Philadelphia: Westminster, 1987); Gordon Fee and Douglas Stuart, *How to Read the Bible for All Its Worth* (Grand Rapids: Zondervan, 1982), 214; and Michael Fox, *Qoheleth and His Contradictions,* Journal for the Study of the Old Testament Series 71, Bible and Literature Series 18 (Sheffield: Almond, 1989).

3. Graham Ogden, *Qoheleth* (Sheffield: JSOT Press, 1987).

4. Roland Murphy, *Ecclesiastes,* Word Biblical Commentary 23A (Dallas: Word, 1992).

5. Edward Good, *Irony in the Old Testament* (Philadelphia: Westminster, 1965), 171.

6. Carol A. Newsom, "Job and Ecclesiastes," in *Old Testament Interpretation: Past, Present, and Future,* ed. James Luther Mays, David L. Petersen, and Kent Harold Richards (Nashville: Abingdon, 1995), 189. Cf. Craig Bartholomew, "Qoheleth in the Canon?! Current Trends in the Interpretation of Ecclesiastes," *Themelios* 24, no. 3 (May 1999): 13; "The failure of twentieth century scholars to reach any kind of consensus about its meaning . . ." Or Sven Holm-Nielsen, "On the Interpretation of Qoheleth in Early Christianity," *Vetus Testamentum* 24, no. 2 (1974): 168: "It is fair to say that no other book in the Old Testament has been interpreted in so radically different ways as the Book of Ecclesiastes."

7. Johannes Pedersen, *Scepticisme Israelite* (Paris: Felix Alcan, 1931), quoted in Murphy, *Ecclesiastes,* 55. Cf. Crenshaw, *Ecclesiastes,* 47: "Research into the book also shows that it reflects the interpreter's worldview. That is why, I think, opinions vary widely with regard to such matters as Qoheleth's optimism or pessimism."

8. Jacques Ellul, *Reason for Being: A Meditation on Ecclesiastes,* trans. Joyce Main Hanks (Grand Rapids: Eerdmans, 1990), 207.

Appendix B

1. Ted Baehr, *What Can We Watch Tonight? A Family Guide to Movies* (Grand Rapids: Zondervan, 2003).

2. E.g., Clive Marsh and Gaye Ortiz, eds., *Explorations in Theology and Film: Movies and Meaning* (Oxford: Blackwell, 1997); and John R. May, ed., *New Images of Religious Film* (Kansas City: Sheed & Ward, 1997). Andrew Greeley and Albert Bergesen, *God in the Movies* (New Brunswick, N.J.: Transaction, 2000). Cf., also, the discussion of theological criticism in Joel W. Martin and Conrad E. Ostwald Jr., *Screening the Sacred: Religion, Myth, and Ideology in Popular American Film* (Boulder: Westview, 1995).

3. E.g., Craig Detweiler and Barry Taylor, *A Matrix of Meanings: Finding God in Pop Culture* (Grand Rapids: Baker Academic, 2003); and Gareth Higgins, *How Movies Helped My Soul: Finding Fingerprints of Faith in Culturally Significant Films* (Lake Mary, Fla.: Relevant Books, 2003).

4. Peter Malone, with Rose Pacatte, *Lights Camera . . . Faith! A Movie Lover's Guide to Scripture,* 3 vols. (Boston: Pauline Books and Media, 2001, 2002, 2003).

5. Doug Fields and Eddie James, *Videos That Teach* (Grand Rapids: Zondervan, Youth Specialties, 1999); and idem, *Videos That Teach 2* (Grand Rapids: Zondervan, Youth Specialties, 2002).

6. E.g., Edward McNulty, *Films and Faith: Forty Discussion Guides* (Topeka: Viaticum Press, 1999); Sarah Anson Vaux, *Finding Meaning at the Movies* (Nashville: Abingdon, 1999); and Catherine Barsotti and Robert K. Johnston, *Finding God in the Movies: 33 Movies of Reel Faith* (Grand Rapids: Baker, 2004).

7. E.g., Ken Gire, *Reflections on the Movies: Hearing God in the Unlikeliest of Places* (Colorado Springs: Chariot Victor, 2000); Edward McNulty, *Praying the Movies* (Louisville: Geneva Press, 2001); and idem, *Praying the Movies II* (Louisville: Westminster John Knox, 2003).

8. E.g., David S. Cunningham, *Reading Is Believing: The Christian Faith through Literature and Film* (Grand Rapids: Brazos, 2002); and Bryan P. Stone, *Faith and Film: Theological Themes at the Cinema* (St. Louis: Chalice, 2000).

9. Larry Kreitzer, *The New Testament in Fiction and Film: On Reversing the Hermeneutical Flow* (Sheffield: Sheffield Academic Press, 1993).

10. Robert Jewett, *St. Paul at the Movies: The Apostle's Dialogue with American Culture* (Louisville: Westminster John Knox, 1993).

Appendix C

1. Cf. Giles Gunn, "Introduction: Literature and Its Relation to Religion," in *Literature and Religion*, ed. Giles Gunn (New York: Harper & Row, 1971), 1–33.

2. For a wider discussion of these four approaches to the biblical text, see Robert K. Johnston, "Interpreting Scripture, Literary Criticism, and Evangelical Hermeneutics," *Christianity and Literature* 32, no. 1 (fall 1982): 33–47.

3. Carol Newsom, "Job and Ecclesiastes," in *Old Testament Interpretation: Past, Present, and Future*, ed. James Luther Mays, David L. Petersen, and Kent Harold Richards (Nashville: Abingdon, 1995), 184.

MOVIES CITED

Wall Street (d. Stone, 1987), 60
Waterboy, The (d. Coraci, 1998), 89
White (d. Kieslowski, 1994), 94
Wide Awake (d. Shyamalan, 1998), 139
Wintersleepers (d. Tykver, 1997), 94

Yojimbo (d. Kurosawa, 1961), 39

INDEX

205